University of Brighton

St Peter's House Library
Telephone 01273 643220

Please return or renew on or before the last date stamped
A fine may be charged if items are returned late

Uncanny Australia

Sacredness and Identity in a Postcolonial Nation

KEN GELDER AND JANE M. JACOBS

MELBOURNE UNIVERSITY PRESS

Melbourne University Press
PO Box 278, Carlton South, Victoria 3053, Australia

First published 1998

Text © Kenneth Douglas Gelder and Jane Margaret Jacobs 1998
Design and typography © Melbourne University Press 1998

Typeset in Malaysia by Syarikat Seng Teik Sdn. Bhd. in Sabon 10/13 point
Printed in Malaysia by SRM Production Services Sdn. Bhd.

National Library of Australia Cataloguing-in-Publication entry

Gelder, Kenneth.
    Uncanny Australia: sacredness and identity in a postcolonial nation.
    Bibliography.
    Includes index.
    ISBN 0 522 84816 8.
    1. National characteristics, Australian. 2. Holy, The. 3. Sacred space.
    4. Aborigines, Australian—Religion. 5. Postcolonialism.
    6. Australia—History—20th century. I. Jacobs, J. M. (Jane Margaret).
    II. Title.
299.9215

'We always knew that the dismantling of the colonial paradigm would release strange demons from the deep.'

Stuart Hall (1996)

'The space inhabited by indeterminate subjects will never be harmonious: a democracy is not a utopia.'

Joan Copjec (1994)

'I believe that the concept of home is a compelling notion in our psyche.'

Prime Minister John Howard (1997)

Contents

Illustrations

Acknowledgements

W E GRATEFULLY acknowledge institutional support which has helped us gather much of the material for this book, and more besides. The Australia Research Council was generous to us in 1992 and 1993, as was the University of Melbourne's Faculty of Arts in early 1996 and 1997. We also thank Tanja Luckins, Mary Quilty, Sue Jackson and Fiona Nicoll for their excellent research assistance, and Chandra Jayasuriya for her wonderful cartographic skills. Thanks to those who read parts or all of the manuscript and offered helpful comments: Tim Rowse, Dipesh Chakrabarty, Simon During, Barry Hill and Kerryn Goldsworthy. Thanks, also, to Teresa Pitt and Gabby Lhuede from Melbourne University Press and our editor, Lee White, for their support for and work on this book. Finally, we are ever grateful to Hannah and Christian for giving us the time and space to put *Uncanny Australia* together.

We would like to thank Routledge for their permission to reproduce a long passage from Bill Readings, *Introducing Lyotard: Art and Politics* (1991).

Introduction

On Discourses of the Sacred, Minorities and Fair Deals

THIS IS A BOOK which analyses how the Aboriginal sacred has been talked about. We take indigenous claims for sacred sites and sacred objects over the last twenty years as crucial in the recasting of Australia's sense of itself. But let us be clear that our book is not about the Aboriginal sacred as some kind of thing-in-itself; we shall not be delving 'anthropologically' into the content of Aboriginal sacred beliefs and practices. Rather, our concern is with what we might call the 'discourses of the sacred': that is, the ways in which Aboriginal sacredness manifests itself in the public domain of a modern nation. We can see these discourses as an *effect* of the Aboriginal sacred, which can draw various parties indiscriminately into the mix: some in sympathy, some in opposition, some directly (Aboriginal people themselves, politicians and bureaucrats, mining personnel, pastoralists, anthropologists, journalists, conservationists, and so on), and some who become affiliated to the Aboriginal sacred under the most indirect and tangential circumstances imaginable.

The indirect—but no less important—aspects of this latter kind of affiliation were brought home to us when we visited the Old Swan Brewery site (Goonininup) in Perth in 1993 as part of a research trip. There had been Aboriginal opposition to planned redevelopment at the site since 1986, most visibly through on-site protests organised by a local Nyunga group called Fringe Dwellers of the Swan Valley who were concerned about protecting a resting place of the Dreamtime creature, Waugal. But when we arrived at the Old Swan Brewery site one morning, the Aboriginal protesters and their various non-Aboriginal sympathisers had gone. All that remained was one man and his car, above which was hoisted an upside-down Australian flag. This man was not Aboriginal, but he had been protesting alongside the Fringe Dwellers because he, too, wanted to stop development and see the Brewery demolished. Yet the reason behind his protest could not have been more different. He told us that the building itself transgressed the sanctity of the foreshore on which it was situated—because that foreshore, for him, uncannily resembled what he called the 'beachhead' of Anzac Cove. The Brewery was situated between the King's Park War Memorial and the Swan River: it broke up the connection between these two sites, interfering with the symbolic resonance (as he saw it) between monument and topography. What was fascinating about this man's protest—and he had written many times to local newspapers and relevant government departments about his concerns—was that it was consistent with the interests of the Aboriginal protest (they both wanted the same outcome), and yet at the same time absolutely incommensurable with those interests. His sympathies appeared to be with the Fringe Dwellers, but he had no direct interest in protecting the sites of Waugal. The protesters did not compete with each other, but neither did they converge. So his affiliation with the Fringe Dwellers is entirely incidental: he is 'with' them, but in a certain sense he doesn't 'see' them. Indeed, this man's protest was utterly idiosyncratic, since it spoke for nothing more or less than his own interests: even the local Returned and Services League (RSL) had disdained him, for example. Yet at the same time, the form of his protest invoked the nation itself. He talked reverently of the Anzac tradition, yet he flew the Australian flag upside-down. He invoked the nation because he felt it, too, had disdained him—making him 'marginal' enough to come out in sympathy with Aboriginal protesters.

The Aboriginal sacred always throws up questions to do with who is 'marginal'—who is empowered enough to claim to represent the nation, and who feels as if the nation has disdained them. Can a wealthy multinational mining company become 'marginal' in contemporary Australia? Can pastoralists—the most powerful of all social groups to emerge out of colonial Australian conditions—feel suddenly embattled, as if no one is listening to them? Can previously obscure parties suddenly become prominent and influential while the prominent and influential find themselves becoming obscured? In which case, who can claim to represent the nation? To put this another way: how can we tell the difference between the idiosyncratic and the emblematic?

In our view, Australia is in a predicament in which these distinctions can never be settled properly. Even majorities can feel that they are precariously placed. In a response to an appeal by the Wik and Thayorre people of Cape York, the High Court in December 1996 ruled, in a 4:3 majority, that pastoral leases do not extinguish native title. Is a 4:3 majority really a majority? For pastoralists in the area who felt unexpectedly overruled by this outcome and fought tooth and nail to change it, apparently not. And yet Australians are governed under a similar ratio, through the rise of a 'convergence politics' that sees the two major political parties increasingly resembling each other and drawing similarly proportioned endorsements from the voting public. So in this sense, the *Wik* decision is quite properly reflective of Australia's contemporary political condition. But whereas a political electoral outcome of 4:3 means a settled majority under which we are then governed, a legal decision of the same proportions in relation to Aboriginal claims brings with it only unsettlement. Such outcomes always seem to require further clarification: decisions are appealed against, claimants are interrogated, testimonies are required, other avenues are actively sought. The intention, it would seem, is to try to clarify the distinction between the 'minority' and the 'majority'. In the process, however, new levels of visibility are attained, new affiliations are made, a kind of amplification occurs, and the boundaries dividing 'minorities' from 'majorities' are often unsettled all the more. Is to become a 'minority' then to be in a position of loss—or gain? Can it actually be helpful to claim an identity as a 'minority' under these conditions? It can seem to be so. This is, no doubt, why conservative forces in Australia continually invest in the notion that, in the wake of innumerable so-called 'single interest' claims on the nation's attention, the 'mainstream' has been forgotten: that 'all of us' have, in fact, become a 'minority' which can then only imagine itself (as minorities so often do) as embattled.

We take the Aboriginal sacred—the claims made about it, the effects it has on others, on democratic rights ('equal opportunities', 'justice for all', etc.), on the nation itself—as a sign of a predicament in modern Australia which we can characterise as postcolonial. This is not just because Aboriginal people have gained some power as a political force in this country over the last twenty or more years, which enables them actually to make a claim for sacredness and expect it at least to register. It is also because of what a claim for Aboriginal sacredness puts into motion: the not-always-predictable character of the affiliations and alliances, the unruly nature of the outcomes and the strange inversions that these claims activate, whereby, for instance, a 'majority' can very well represent itself as a 'minority' and, conversely, a 'minority' can very well end up speaking on behalf of the nation. Our book is also concerned with another consequence of Aboriginal claims for sacredness which we can note here: to turn what seems like 'home' into something else, something less familiar and less settled. This is one meaning of the term 'uncanny', which we shall elaborate in detail in Chapter 2. Our book thus charts modern Australia's entanglement with its sacred sites and sacred objects: willing or unwilling, as the case may be. We want to look at what effects the Aboriginal sacred in its modern context unleashes across the nation (enthralment, irritation, downright anxiety), and how certain people, in turn, variously talk it up or try to close it down; or rather, as so often happens in the case of some of these people, *talk it up even as they try to close it down*. Our book may appear to map modern Australia through specific sites over which Aboriginal claims have been made, such as Coronation Hill, Uluru, Kow Swamp and Hindmarsh Island. But, in fact, these sites are never just discrete 'sites' (just as minorities are never just 'minorities'), because of the claims and counter-claims made upon them by various affiliated parties. The very exclusivity claimed for these sites makes them somehow radiate across the nation and beyond, so that to speak about Coronation Hill a few years ago was also to speak about Canberra, as well as global business interests which operated in Australia as well as elsewhere.

Who can be drawn into the frame of the Aboriginal sacred? Who can make proper, or improper, use of provisions for Aboriginal claims over (for example) land? Let us note one more strange manifestation of the current predicament in order to demonstrate simply just how unpredictable these affiliations can be. In October 1996 the Melbourne *Age* reported that William Hollier, a man of non-Aboriginal descent, was planning to lodge a claim for Deal Island in Bass Strait under the Native Title Act.[1] Hollier is an environmental scientist who has lived on the island with his family, as the sole occupants, for the past four years—not long in the Aboriginal scheme of things. Nevertheless, with no evidence of prior Aboriginal occupation of the island, Hollier felt enabled enough, or indigenous enough, to make a claim for its possession. Was he simply appropriating Native Title provisions for his own interests? Or was this an entirely unexpected example of convergence, drawing otherwise discrete groups together? Hollier naturally enough saw things in the latter terms, telling the reporter: 'I am not trying to reduce the effectiveness of native title. I am trying to enhance it'. The boundaries between minority provisions and majority access are certainly confused here. The newspaper headline ran the following most appropriate pun: 'Scientist appeals for fair Deal'. This man wanted to authorise his occupation of Deal Island through an uncanny procedure whereby it was impossible to tell whether he was 'Aboriginalising' his whiteness or whitening legislation which is specifically Aboriginal. It spoke both to enthralment (in the sense that this man wished to replicate Aboriginal relations to land) and disdain (in the sense that he flowed over into those relations only to draw them back to his own advantage). The *Age*'s pun was appropriate because this man's action was on the one hand democratic, in that one person wanted the same opportunities and rights as another, while on the other hand it was transgressive, in that in the process it diluted another group's distinctiveness. And notice the absolutely uncanny feature of that former point (a feature we shall return to elsewhere in this book): that a non-Aboriginal man wants exactly the same opportunities and rights as Aboriginal people. A non-Aboriginal man wants to be 'indigenous' enough to actually use Native Title as a way of legitimating his claim to country! This was, as it happens, a feature imaginatively put to use in Rob Sitch's popular film *The Castle* (1997), a light comedy which has a white suburban family invoke the precedent of the *Mabo* decision to secure—in the High Court, no less—their own property rights to a home from which they are about to be dispossessed.

These otherwise idiosyncratic events speak to a condition which manifests itself in a peculiar way in postcolonial Australia: that democracy, as a political system which continually imagines that it speaks for 'all of us' as if we do all have equal opportunities and rights, is never fully reconcilable with itself. Indeed, we can take up the very topic of 'reconciliation' in this context. Was Hollier's claim on Deal Island an example of Aboriginal and non-Aboriginal convergence, of the kind 'reconciliation' seems to speak and hope for? Or is 'reconciliation' always shadowed by the sense of transgression and appropriation that this example carries with it? Our book wants to suggest that reconciliation is never a fully realisable category; it can never be completely settled. For a nation which continues to invest in reconciliation, albeit often falteringly, this may not be good news. But let us instead take unsettlement—the kind of unsettlement that a claim on a sacred site or object can give rise to, for example—as a productive feature of the postcolonial landscape. It incites discourses and counter-discourses; it produces alignments and realignments; most of all, it reminds us that (whether we like it or not) 'all of us' are implicated to greater or lesser degrees in this modern predicament. In other words, we want to give unsettlement an activating function. But let us also remember just how fragile this predicament can be. An Aboriginal claim for sacredness, particularly when it involves a claim for land, is always conflictual, and this can lead as much to restriction as it can to activation. In response to such claims boundaries are established, administrations (which can often seem neocolonial rather than postcolonial) are put into place, and limits are set. Yet even so, activation persists, and it is this persistence to which our book pays tribute.

As we noted at the beginning of this introduction, we shall mostly be analysing ways in which the Aboriginal sacred has been talked about. We need to emphasise the point that this often secret thing is, in fact, talked about incessantly, with the boundaries between the secret and the public being constantly renegotiated (which was a feature of relations between colonials and Aboriginal people, too). Our book, then, is full of examples of what people have been saying about the Aboriginal sacred. Let us just make two points about this feature. Firstly, it seems to us that this incessant chatter about the sacred is something to be relished, even when that chatter elicits concern and/or disapproval. This may well be considered as another manifestation of the entanglement of incitement (to talk) and restraint (to attempt, at least, to talk 'properly') just mentioned. So one of the methods we use in our book involves returning what has been said about sacredness back to the reader: our book is full of very quotable quotes, in other words. Secondly, in order to bring all this chatter together, we have moved across a wide range of texts from various implicated parties: Aboriginal narratives, mining industry statements, media reportage, literature, political commentaries, feature films, documentaries and academic interpretations from a number of disciplines. We treat these texts as being entangled in their own way, too, in the sense that we regard all of them as equally idiosyncratic/emblematic in relation to the predicament we are outlining.

The Modern Sacred

On the New Age of a
Postcolonial Nation

S OME OF US may think of Aboriginal sacredness as anachronistic in a modern, secularised nation state such as Australia. It can seem as if modernity has somehow left it behind, as if—at a time when 'nothing is sacred'—sacredness can only be conceived of nostalgically, as something good which has been 'lost' and which at best exists only as a residue in the form of heritage sites or preserved objects. And yet Aboriginal sacredness figures much more largely, and insistently, in this country these days. Far from being left behind as a relic or as a residue, it may even be able to determine aspects of Australia's future; far from being out of place in Australia, it sometimes seems (to an increasing number of commentators) to be *all over the place*. There is no doubt that the Aboriginal sacred continues to impact upon modern Australia, not least because claims are still being made for it. Indeed, a claim for a sacred site in Australia these days is nothing less than a modern phenomenon; the relationship between Aboriginal sacredness and modernity may be more intimate than first might be imagined.

We can see this clearly in two apparently distinct spheres of modern Australian life. On the one hand, much contemporary New Age environmentalism and Jungian spiritualism turns to Aboriginal religion as a means of making modernity reconcilable with itself. Here, Aboriginal sacredness retains its other-worldly, residual features, but it is also activated as something emergent, as integral to what we might (or should) 'become'. It is precisely because Aboriginal sacredness appears so out-of-step with modernity that it is able to be identified as the very thing modernity needs. On the other hand, Aboriginal sacredness is also a fact of modern, bureaucratic life: worldly, rather than other-worldly. It is continually being dealt with by governments, businesses, mining companies and mediators. For many of these interests, Aboriginal sacredness is, to invoke properly a set of terms taken from Raymond Williams, neither residual nor emergent, but dominant.[1] It is a bit *too* active for their liking and precisely the thing that modernity (as it routinely encourages economic development and fusses over its budgets) does not need. As a commentator from the Institute of Public Affairs, Ron Brunton, put it in an article on the Hindmarsh Island dispute in South Australia, Aboriginal claims for sacredness are 'blocking business'.[2] From this commonplace perspective, sacredness needs to be deactivated, discouraged, restrained; the sites themselves need to be identified only in order to be restricted, bounded, fenced off: neutralised.

New Age-ism turns to Aboriginal sacredness for quite opposite reasons in that, far from 'blocking business', it would seem to be able to unblock the impasse of modernity itself. Under this logic modernity represses our innate, latent spirituality, which needs to be recovered and brought out into the open. So it appears, then, as if New Age-ism releases the sacred, whereas business and government interests work to restrain it. And yet it is in the latter's management of the sacred that something quite peculiar occurs—where, even at the very moment of its restraint, Aboriginal sacredness is capable of generating effects far beyond the boundaries ascribed to it. If the identification of a sacred site was merely a way of underscoring its residual or marginal character, and thereby managing or restraining it, then Western Mining magnate Hugh Morgan would not have felt compelled to say that the Hawke government's recognition of Coronation Hill as a sacred site in 1991 was a 'shocking defeat' for the nation, similar in proportions to the fall of Singapore in 1942![3] Nor would Professor John R. Burton from the University of New England have been so shaken by this decision as to wonder not only about the state of the nation but, more particularly, about the impact upon his own pedagogical practices: 'What have we come to? . . . Where are we heading? . . . And what am I going to tell my students in the future?'.[4] We need not imagine that these are entirely untypical responses to the impact of Aboriginal sacredness on the nation's fortunes. Nor need we imagine they are confined to maverick right-wingers who become somehow unrepresentative or idiosyncratic through their male hysterics. Indeed, as this book continues, we shall inquire further into the implications of what we might think of here as a mode of 'white moral panic' which has been quite widespread and which, far from presuming that the sacred is a constrained, deactivated thing, blames modernity itself for its very unleashing. So, although they seem poles apart, New Age-ism and business or government interests have this feature in common. They both participate in the activation of Aboriginal sacredness; indeed, they are both drawn to the sacred (willingly or unwillingly, wittingly or unwittingly) and are thus compelled to represent it not as residual or marginal, but as something of profound significance, something whose significance extends well beyond its actual locality which may itself be 'insignificant'. Think of the actual locations of Coronation Hill or Hindmarsh Island (sites which we shall discuss in subsequent chapters) in this respect, and then think of how those locations have been put to use, how they have become invested with such significance that they can even seem iconic: standing for ever so much more than the mere place itself would suggest (which is, in fact, a way of expressing exactly what it means for a place to be a sacred site).

Our book is written as a response to this feature: that these days a claim for Aboriginal sacredness is also a claim on what would otherwise seem to be a modern, secular nation; that a 'minor' event is so often figured in 'major' ways and given a beneficial or a negative identity as a consequence, depending on the case. This is a book about, precisely, the 'modern sacred', about how these two otherwise distinct things become entangled with each other, to such an extent that it would seem (at least in Australia's case) that they cannot live apart.

There has been a longstanding interest in the place of the sacred in the modern world, and it is worth pausing at the outset to draw attention to some key figures who have helped to shape the way this can be thought about. A range of disciplines have been involved in this ongoing discussion—religious history, anthropology, social theory, and so on—and what they have to say may seem strangely familiar to us in contemporary Australia. We can begin by looking at a text which marked a transition from anthropology to sociology and drew directly upon studies of Australian Aboriginal people: Emile Durkheim's *The Elementary Forms of the Religious Life* (1915). Durkheim's project was to examine Aboriginal religion, Aboriginal sacredness in particular, in order to understand modernity better, in order to speak directly to the modern condition. In other words, he gave it an activated role, becoming intimate with it so that it could function not just as a residual thing but as an emergent, embodied presence: 'our task', he says, 'has as its object the explanation of some actual reality which is *near to us*, and which consequently is capable of affecting our ideas and our acts . . .'[5] Durkheim also recognised that it is the very nature of modernity which directed his attention to Aboriginal religion—to what he designates as the 'primitive'—in the first place. For Durkheim, the sacred is central to religion, and it works to organise people socially; it unites them '*into one single moral community*'.[6] This is a fundamental insight for Durkheim: that sacredness produces sociality. This connection is realised through a study of Aboriginal religion and then applied to the modern world, which must be reminded of the sociality it now seems to lack. This is why, for Durkheim, the otherwise 'primitive' phenomenon of sacredness must always be 'near to us'. Its profound significance lies in the fact that it stands for something—the *social*—which seems increasingly difficult to grasp in the modern world.

This thesis puts Durkheim in a particular quandary in that he runs the risk of making the 'primitive' seem consequently more attractive than the modern, a feature we see today in much New Age-ism. There is certainly some nostalgia here, but Durkheim is also at pains to say that he does not wish to ascribe 'particular virtues to the lower religions': 'we cannot make of them', he remarks, 'a sort of model which later religions only have to reproduce'.[7] For Durkheim, the 'primitive' remains an elementary thing which, although it is 'near to us', must nevertheless continue to be distinguished from the modern world. The connection between the 'primitive' and the elementary is crucial to this point. By contrast modernity is described in terms of 'the development of *luxury*'.[8] So modernity stands in a super-structural relationship to the base of the 'primitive'; Durkheim even describes the 'primitive' as that 'nude' thing that modernity clothes.[9] But as soon as this distinction is offered, he compromises it in two ways. Firstly, the clothing that modernity provides is sometimes transparent, a feature he relies on in order to be able to look at the 'primitive' in the first place. Secondly, and more importantly for us, Durkheim concedes that the 'primitive' can also be a 'luxurious' thing: 'But that is not equivalent to saying that all luxury is lacking to the primitive cults'.[10] So modernity is in one breath seen to have something extra, something more than the 'primitive'—which is lacking. And yet he also concedes that the 'primitive' does *not* lack; that it, too, can have that something extra which otherwise defines modernity for him. The 'primitive' can also be a luxurious thing.

The paradox of this position is nicely expressed in Durkheim's subsequent description of what he calls 'the lower religions' as 'rudimentary and gross'. At first glance, this description would seem simply to stabilise the 'primitive' status of Aboriginal religion. But, in fact, these two words flatly contradict each other. 'Rudimentary' means elemental or undeveloped, a definition which maintains the sense that 'primitive' religion is not modern. But 'gross' means luxuriant, flagrant or excessive; in which case, it has quite the opposite implication. In other words, this description of so-called 'primitive' religions as 'rudimentary and gross' suggests lack and plenitude at the same time, both distinguishing the 'primitive' from the modern and yet allowing it to overflow into modernity on the grounds that it, too, can be a luxurious thing. We can write the following equation for this strange paradox: the 'primitive' is (not) modern.

So Durkheim gives us two senses of Aboriginal religion, as well as the sacred which is for him religion's 'vital substance'.[11] Firstly, he establishes the proximity of the sacred to the modern world: it is 'near to us'; we can become intimate with it; it speaks directly to 'the man of to-day'.[12] He may have wanted to distinguish the sacred from modernity; but in the process, he gives it such a radical instability ('rudimentary' and yet 'gross') that it seems at times as if it is modernity's mirror image. Secondly, and this follows on from the first point, Durkheim endows the sacred with immense significance.

Far from imagining the sacred as a 'primitive' residue or an anachronistic remainder, it provides modernity with an image of what it might become. The sacred is a socialising force; it provides the 'very concept of totality' which takes the modern individual beyond 'his own narrow horizon',[13] beyond a modern condition which is defined, paradoxically here, as a lack. The paradox lies in this fact: that modernity, which is a 'luxurious' thing, is nevertheless seen to be lacking when it is without the sacred. The sacred is 'something [which is] added to and above the real':[14] in this sense, like modernity it, too, is super-structural. For Durkheim, the modern individual is restricted by the limits of his interior life; the sacred, which enables the social to realise itself, 'raises' the individual into the exterior, vital realm of the group. The sacred, which might otherwise have been designated as 'primitive', thus becomes *the luxury that the modern world cannot afford to do without*.

Let us pause momentarily over this conclusion and place it, somewhat casually for the moment, in the context of modern Australia and Aboriginal claims for sacred sites. How often are such claims seen, by mining companies, businesses and governments, as luxuries we simply cannot afford!

Twenty years after Durkheim's study—and remaining in France for a moment longer—Georges Bataille, Roger Caillois, the surrealist Michel Leiris and others returned to the question of the relationship between sacredness and the modern world. Disillusioned with modernity, and complaining that contemporary studies of old religions were irrelevant insofar as they relegated sacredness to a 'primitive' and remote sphere, they developed what they called a 'sacred sociology' in an attempt to bring these two realms back together again. These people owe a great deal to Durkheim, in the sense that they too credit sacredness with a social force in what they see to be an otherwise disintegrating modern world. Nevertheless, there are some important differences which we would like to elaborate here, as they give further insights into how we might think about the Aboriginal sacred in Australia today.

We want to begin by returning to the issue of luxury. For Bataille, in particular, 'primitive' religion was distinguished from modern capitalism in that the latter is built upon acquisition (the attainment of luxury) while the former involved ritualised sacrifice and excessive expenditure; that is, it was already luxurious. Precapitalist religions were, in fact, so luxurious that they were able to measure wealth through its dissipation: 'Wealth is determined not by what one retains in reserve but by what one *squanders*'.[15] In *The Accursed Share* (first published in 1967) Bataille turns to Durkheim's nephew Marcel Mauss's seminal study of 'primitive' forms of economy, *The Gift* (1950), to elaborate on this point. Bataille draws attention first and foremost to the question of expenditure, to what he describes as the 'joy' of giving excessive amounts, more than is required, more than is 'useful'. In this economy of luxury, one gives, and continues to give, and so becomes charismatic: charisma derives from squandering wealth. One sacrifices and squanders in a luxurious, 'extreme' way, and in doing so produces sociality—which is held together by charismatic forces. Modern society, by contrast, simply accumulates wealth; it is retentive in this respect; it blocks the possibility of social cohesion.

Bataille and his colleagues turn to the sacred in order to unblock that blockage: to make social cohesion a modern possibility. But the problem for them—not being postcolonial, not living amongst Aboriginal claims for sacredness as contemporary Australians do—is one of identification: what exactly *is* the sacred? How did they begin to speak about the social force of the sacred? The view that modern society was lacking amounted to seeing it as emasculated, in which case the sacred was seen to be able to supply what was missing here: virility. Quoting Bataille, Denis Hollier describes their infatuation with virility in his introduction to *The College of Sociology (1937–39)* (1989):

'The creation of the vital bond between men' therefore, is the remedy proposed against the modern detumescence of the social. A man is never alone. To be a man is to be united. Virility is the social bond . . . Virility, the experience of what [Bataille] called full existence, was contrasted with the different forms of [modern] emptiness.[16]

It is difficult to imagine ascribing the sacred with a more active role than this: for these sacred sociologists, it stands for nothing less than the phallus. The modern world, by contrast, is 'devirilised', unmanned, uncharismatic. Flirting with both fascism and communism, Bataille and his colleagues blame two things in particular for this predicament: democracy and the literary genre of the novel. Both of these things—and the novel is cast as democracy's symptomatic mode of expression—divide rather than unite, individualise rather than socialise, regulate rather than lose themselves in forms of 'extreme' expenditure. They are 'post-sacred' forms: the sacred has gone from them: they are, in fact, actually responsible for 'the draining away of the sacred'.[17]

The project of these 'sacred sociologists', accordingly, was to try to reactivate the sacred, to return it as a luxurious thing to what they saw as an otherwise depleted modernity. And yet they also find themselves in Durkheim's predicament, where it seems at the same time as if the sacred is already there. Michel Leiris, for example, spoke about 'my sacred' in a lecture titled 'The sacred in everyday life' (1938). Here, he links the sacred to his childhood memories, not as something distant but something of which he is in full possession ('I see forming bit by bit an image of what, for me, is the *sacred*').[18] Leiris seems here to have entirely forgotten about the College's idea of the sacred as a social force, individualising it as a unique, personal memory. This aside, his lecture is built around the thesis that the sacred is not an absence in modern life at all, but a presence. It no longer stands in contrast to a profane modernity; rather, it circulates through it as if has been there all the time. Denis Hollier draws attention to this feature of the sacred, that it is seen by these people as 'absent' and 'omnipresent' at the same time: it has no place (in modernity), and yet it is all over the place. Hollier points to what he calls the 'essential attribute' of the sacred in this respect: its 'ambivalence'.[19]

We can see the relevance of Durkheim, Bataille and others to the Australian context when, for example, we come to look closely at contemporary New Age and Jungian commentaries on sacredness in the nation. David Tacey's *The Edge of the Sacred: Transformation in Australia* (1995) has become a key text in this field. We might imagine that such interventions are speaking to marginal interests; but, as if to remind us that the marginal always exceeds its marginality, when he was Labor Prime Minister Paul Keating was said to have recommended this particular book to his Cabinet as required reading. So *The Edge of the Sacred* was given a certain centrality by official culture. The book was seen as a visionary statement on Australia's modern condition and the counsel it gave is still taken seriously by many commentators. This is why, in the light of our previous discussion, we would like to look closely at this book and the claims it makes.

First of all we should note that David Tacey is not a sociologist and so does not draw quite the same connection between the sacred and society that we have seen above. Nevertheless, the sacred is given a healing force which can transform society and draw 'all of us' together. Tacey is a Jungian commentator who describes the national condition in terms of the psychic relationship between the unconscious and the ego. These categories are associated respectively with sacredness and the modern world. The problem for Tacey lies in the way that the one can overrule or dominate the other. The modern world can certainly overrule sacredness, to the extent of banishing it from its domain, and it is this absence of sacredness in modern Australian life which worries Tacey the most. But he also feels that sacredness can overrule the modern world in return. The ego must not be 'swamped by the unconscious'; the latter should not be absent, but it should not be omnipresent either. Australians, he says, must 'learn to live in the presence of the sacred without being overwhelmed by it'.[20] This proposition, that the ego and the unconscious must not overwhelm each other, makes it clear that Tacey's book is addressed directly to a form of reconciliation— although he never gives this any clear political articulation. This is the 'transformation' that Tacey is advocating and which, no doubt, made the book seem so relevant to a Prime Minister for whom reconciliation seemed to provide the means by which Australia could become 'one nation' (cf. Durkheim's 'one single moral community').

So for Tacey, reconciliation is built around the fruitful interaction of the unconscious and the ego, the sacred and the modern world. They should come together but through a process of restraint, each knowing their place. The modern world should learn humility before the sacred, so that sacredness will not, in turn, be overwhelming. The problem for what is otherwise an idiosyncratic expression of 'sustainable development'—and Tacey is a kind of environmentalist, too—is that the sacred and the modern world, the unconscious and the ego, do not always know their place. Unlike Bataille, Tacey stands against excess, seeing its squandering potential negatively rather than positively. The modern world in particular seems to Tacey to be underwritten by excessive behaviours. For example, it is riven by what he calls 'patriarchal excess' and 'extreme masculinity': far from being 'devirilised', it has too much virility![21] At the other end of the spectrum, feminism and other politically oppositional social forces are seen as equally unrestrained: Tacey also speaks against what he calls 'the excesses and indulgences of the matriarchal counter-culture'.[22] It is important to grasp here that, in Tacey's view, modernity has opened itself up to a whole range of excesses precisely because it has banished the sacred:

> The psyche, like nature, abhors a vacuum, and the vacuum . . . has invited into the soul a plethora of religious and archetypal images. This metaphysical 'inundation' has coincided with, and been furthered by, the enormous explosions and developments of modern technology, whose 'information highway' and commercial productions have made available virtually every religious tradition, cult, or cosmology known to human history. In society, countless numbers of symbolic and mythological systems are for sale in the new age supermarket.[23]

Another critic (one more sympathetic to globalisation, one less caught up with the problem of 'national identity') might very well read this 'inundation' positively, in the sense that it speaks to modernity's capacity to democratise knowledge and increase public access—allowing people to purchase a book like Tacey's from precisely the kind of 'new age supermarket' he is describing. But Tacey reads this 'inundation' negatively, not least because it implies instability and a lack of discipline. He thus speaks with concern about a range of things which seem to typify this predicament: 'the orgy of consumerism', 'the burgeoning drug epidemic', 'promiscuous sexuality', 'forbidden and taboo sexual liaisons' and so on.[24] These things produce a certain amount of anxiety for Tacey since they potentially block his project of sustainable development at the national level. You cannot have 'promiscuity' when you advocate reconciliation because reconciliation relies on settling things down, on stability. It is a formal arrangement involving mutual consent between two partners who are obliged to remain committed to each other, that is, who practise self-restraint. In short, reconciliation is monogamous. It cannot sustain itself in a 'promiscuous' environment where anything goes.

The proliferation of these excessive and promiscuous forms suggests for Tacey that the longing for sacredness is nevertheless still there in modern society. In themselves, however, these forms signify a certain lack of development, as if the sacred is only half-realised, or mis-realised. They are symptoms of a defensive or blocked stance in relation to the sacred. Tacey associates consumerism, promiscuous sex and so on with adolescence, immaturity, impulsiveness: 'Australian society', he says, is 'plagued by [such] negative or inferior expressions'.[25] His account is thus related to the commonplace view that Australia has not yet 'grown up', that it is 'inauthentic' (a word Tacey uses many times), that it is not yet properly civilised, that it has (in relation to the rest of the world?) not yet matured—and, of course, maturity and self-restraint go hand-in-hand in this account. We should note that all of this happens outside the frame of the political, which is itself seen as an underdeveloped, immature response to the world. From his 'psychological' perspective, Tacey has this to say about that most important of contemporary political decisions, the *Mabo* ruling of 1992:[26]

> the new Mabo legislation (*sic*) could almost be read as a defensive and legalistic acting-out of an impulse which is refused realisation at a deeper and more challenging level. It is relatively easy to construct piles of government documents and unreadable official prose in order to fob off or deny the more difficult claims that are being made by the interior indigenous archetypal person.[27]

Let us at least note here the short shrift that 'psychological' readings can give to history: this 'relatively easy' decision took some two hundred years to be realised. (One wonders whether Paul Keating's Cabinet wisely skipped over this particular passage.)

That final phrase in the above quote—'the interior indigenous archetypal person'—alerts us to the central interest of Tacey's book, since it describes the kind of figure he imagines we should all become. The paradox of Tacey's thesis is that an otherwise under-developed modern Australia can achieve (spiritual) development only by turning back to the 'primitive': to Aboriginal religion. Tacey, then, has much in common with Durkheim. The difference between them lies in the fact that Durkheim had equated the sacred with the social, while Tacey finds it through Aboriginal associations with the environment, a sociality-in-Nature. It is not that Aboriginal people are flatly equated with Nature here, although Tacey does seem to get very close to this primitivist position. Rather, Aboriginal people become a conduit through which others can travel to their 'own' spiritual awakening which is itself imagined as a 'primitive' thing: it 'will be "savage" in the sense of being untamed, primordial'.[28] In this respect Tacey again differs from Durkheim in that he does endow Aboriginal religion with enough 'virtue' to provide 'a sort of model which later religions only have to reproduce'.[29] In other words, he is much more nostalgic than Durkheim. For Tacey, one returns to the premodern in order to (re)produce a fully developed modern identity. He is at pains to say, however, that this does not amount to appropriating Aboriginal religion for 'our' purposes. In his account, modern non-Aboriginal Australians are the 'thesis' and Aboriginal people are the 'anti-thesis': one reconciles the two in order to transcend their in-commensurability and thus produce 'synthesis'.[30] This synthesis provides an 'answering image' for non-Aboriginal Australians which mirrors Aboriginal spirituality by creating an 'aboriginal' identity (with a small 'a') which has its own 'dreaming' (with a small 'd').[31]

Let us note how closely aligned synthesis and appropriation really are here. Tacey's 'aboriginal' identity owes everything to the fact that an Aboriginal spirituality precedes it. This is by no means a synthesis between two equal partners, since modern Australian society is viewed as lacking-through-its-excess, inauthentic, empty, etc., whereas Aboriginal spirituality is seen as complete, authentic, full. Tacey endows Aboriginal spirituality with such profound significance that it becomes omnipresent: it fills up this modern emptiness; it is the means by which those modern excesses can be restrained. Is this a form of appropriation? Does modern society take possession of Aboriginal sacredness? Or is modern society possessed by it? Whichever view you take, it is clear that Aboriginal sacredness is given such a profound significance, such empowerment, that it runs the risk of refusing to allow Tacey's reconciliation/ synthesis ever to settle. The sacred, as Tacey imagines it in his book, flows into everything he describes; it is omnipresent; it is, in fact, the book's most 'promiscuous' feature. But having made it so 'promiscuous', Tacey reacts by restraining it in turn, to such an extent that it becomes the opposite of what it was: an absence. The capital 'A' is transformed into a small 'a'. (Aboriginal people, by contrast, have spent a considerable amount of time trying to get others to give their title a capital letter!) This is the 'transformation', then, that Tacey advocates—a transformation that works itself out by effacing the word 'Aboriginal'. A Jungian synthesis may be able to live perfectly well without a capital 'A', but this is a luxury that reconciliation in its political manifestation simply cannot afford to indulge. Tacey privileges the 'psychological': he has nothing to say (apart from an aside on the *Mabo* decision, quoted above) about Aboriginal people and politics. Indeed, his refusal to speak about Aboriginal people politically is precisely what allows him to do away with that capital 'A'. He has empowered them spiritually so that they may transform 'all of us'; after putting them to use in this way, all Tacey appears able to do is leave them behind.

It seems quite strange in the framework of modern Australia to cut Aboriginal people out of the political. Indeed, Australia has become 'postcolonial'—a word Tacey rarely uses—because the claims Aboriginal people (with a capital 'A') make on Australia work themselves out first and foremost in the political sphere. Let us note for the moment how broad this sphere can be and how many interests it can involve: not just political parties, but the judiciary, business, bureaucrats, environmentalists, pastoralists and a range of other special interest groups, as well as various 'aberrant' individuals who manage to get publicity for themselves in the midst of all this. Everyone in Australia feels, at one point or another, suitably qualified to make a political judgement about Aboriginal people. From our point of view, then, the political is as omnipresent as the sacred was for Durkheim, Bataille, Tacey et al. Rather than try to distinguish between them, as if the sacred is somehow an apolitical thing, it would be more realistic to think them through together. And, in fact, the discourses that structure the one—lack, excess, luxury, squandering, restraint, synthesis—are precisely the discourses that structure the other.

This uncanny resemblance is nowhere better illustrated than in events surrounding the 1996 Federal election in Australia. It is quite possible to read the conservative coalition victory in this election, at least to some extent, as an expression of disenchantment with Paul Keating's Labor project of reconciliation, which had commenced as an official political programme in 1992 but was given its strongest expression in the *Mabo* decision and in the Native Title legislation. One feature of the 1996 election was that a number of maverick candidates from both sides of the political spectrum made claims which may well have seemed 'aberrant' but which also appeared to provide an 'answering image' (in Tacey's words) to the sentiments of the majority. A number of politicians from the three major parties—Bob Burgess, Bob Katter, Pauline Hanson (all from Queensland) and Graeme Campbell (Western Australia)—each identified themselves as outspoken 'independent' figures who were able to risk making public claims which were liable to be received as racist. Some of these candidates were subsequently dropped by their parties as if to underline their 'aberrance' or unacceptability; but at the same time the nation endowed these figures with profound significance, reporting on them, profiling them, sometimes agreeing with them, sometimes worrying about them. Burgess had complained that 'Aboriginal communities squandered government grant money on alcohol and gambling'.[32] Katter had (famously) noted that 'children in rural Australia could not complete a secondary-school education unless their parents were either rich or of Aboriginal descent'.[33] Campbell aligned himself with Pauline Hanson, whose case has been by far the most spectacular: her remarks about Aboriginal people being looked after 'too much' by government bureaucrats were taken as the reason why she managed to win what was assumed to be a safe Labor seat. Hanson was promptly dropped by the coalition, which then, when it won the election, went on to legitimate her complaint by focusing its attention on the squandering of public money in the corridors of the Aboriginal and Torres Strait Islander Commission (ATSIC), the bureaucratic wing of Aboriginal people in Australia—and then moved to restrain ATSIC by drastically reducing its budget in order to service the national debt.

It is only recently that Aboriginal people have been accused of having 'too much'—and certainly, it is a novel and contemporary rhetorical ploy to align them, as Katter did, with 'the rich'. It has, of course, been usual to think about Aboriginal people as not having *enough*, as lacking: for example, lacking their land, self-determination, justice, adequate health and housing, and so on. There is certainly no denying that Aboriginal people are radically disadvantaged. But there is also a modern perception which sees Aboriginal people as in receipt of special privileges, that they are the unique beneficiaries of what is often called 'reverse discrimination'. We can note how this perception completely effaces the view, more in tune with our colonial legacy, that Aboriginal people remain disadvantaged: these views are by no means reconciled with one another. So what does it mean when someone equates Aboriginal people with the rich? When someone says they have 'too much'? When they are seen to squander resources in a way which, it seems to be assumed, contrasts to the restraint apparently practised by other modern Australians? Is this a form of racism? For the conservative commentator P. P. McGuinness this is not racism but 'racism': the word does not quite resemble itself any more. McGuinness is, not surprisingly, sympathetic to Katter's claim that white Australians in northern Queensland are the ones who are *really* lacking: 'when you are suffering yourself, and your kids are missing out on an education, resentment and envy are difficult to overcome'.[34] The implication is that people in a position of lack— white Australians in this case, rather than Aboriginal people— cannot be racist, only 'racist'. Other commentators from the Right have moved this along one step further. Aboriginal people, because they are perceived no longer to be lacking, are now capable of being racist in turn, as historian Geoffrey Blainey suggests: 'Australia is now in the curious situation where racism is even praiseworthy if . . . it comes from a minority'.[35] It seems, then, that one can only be racist from a position of abundance: of luxury, of privilege; a position now ascribed, bizarrely enough, to Aboriginal people today.

What this produces is an uncanny inversion which is symptomatic of modern Australia after the *Mabo* decision. The *Mabo* decision and the subsequent Native Title Act of 1993 were built around the overturning of *terra nullius*, the view that Aboriginal people were 'not here', the view that they were an absence in Australia, not in terms of their person, but in terms of property rights. These legal/political provisions recognised instead that Aboriginal people were not only a presence but required a range of compensations to acknowledge that fact. At an earlier point in Australia's modern history Aboriginal people were imagined as owning nothing. But now, especially after *Mabo*, Aboriginal ownership has the potential to reach right across Australia: all over the place. A mining company was once able to indulge in the luxury of ignoring Aboriginal interests; but these days nothing can go ahead until an Aboriginal presence has been properly acknowledged. This radical shift from absence to profound significance produces the 'swing to resentment' that characterises Katter et al.'s complaints.

We have been arguing that the sacred has been imagined through an uncanny association of lack and luxury: in Durkheim's words, it is 'rudimentary and gross'. The current view of Aboriginal people in their political formation is expressed along exactly the same lines. To be in a culture which can see Aboriginal people as lacking and yet having 'too much' at the same time is itself an uncanny phenomenon. We have already suggested that these views take us in contradictory directions—the former returning us to the historical fact of colonialism, and the latter blithely ignoring that fact by living solely in a post-*Mabo* imaginary. The important point for us to emphasise here is that these views are not reconciled with each other—there is no synthesis here—and yet they do somehow live together. They come out of the same contemporary Australian environment. Let us bind these contradictory views together under the title of 'postcolonial racism'. This is a form of racism (and we need not use those inverted commas any more) which sees Aboriginal people as lacking on the one hand—in which case, one will feel sympathy, guilt, shame, etc.[36]—and having 'too much' on the other, in which case one feels 'resentment'. The problem in contemporary Australia is: *at what point does the one become the other?*

We have been observing a crucial feature of postcolonial Australia, namely, that the interests of minorities have been increasingly recognised, credited with a significance that some may feel is more than their 'minority' status deserves. Along with recognition comes empowerment, sometimes at the expense of other, more established organisations which imagine themselves as lacking as a consequence. We have already noted that mining companies in Australia now negotiate with Aboriginal groups about their mutual relations to sacred sites, a fact which would suggest in itself that sacredness is an activated and significant thing. But when mining companies go to court against Aboriginal people, they can be surprised by the amount of power they have actually lost, at least in terms of the way the courts recognise the presence, and the legitimacy, of each party's claims. Going to court, which is where disputes over sacred sites inevitably end up these days, is obviously a tribute to an Aboriginal presence in the nation. Accordingly, both parties find themselves participating in a redistribution of power; one's claim (which may once have gone unrecognised) is now just as legitimate as another's (which may once have been the *only* claim that was recognised). In postcolonial theory, there is a useful term to describe this new condition of poly-legitimacy: the 'differend'. As with much of what is identified as theory, this term has continental origins, introduced by Jean-François Lyotard; but we need not indulge our scepticism simply on these grounds because this term has real uses. For Lyotard, the differend speaks directly to this issue of poly-legitimacy in the law courts: 'As distinguished from a litigation, a differend . . . would be a case of conflict, between (at least) two parties, that cannot be equitably resolved for lack of a rule of judgment applicable to both arguments. One side's legitimacy does not imply the other's lack of legitimacy'.[37] The virtue of this concept is that it captures this very real possibility, that an organisation with a great deal of power may not necessarily come out of the courts with their power intact; while conversely, a group with very little power may be activated through legal recognition—which is precisely what had happened in the 1992 *Mabo* decision to acknowledge legally Aboriginal former occupation of Australia (although it has happened in many land and site disputes, both before *Mabo* and after it). And all this takes place without having to say that one or the other group is wrong, as the differend observes.

However, the problem with the differend is that it retains a sense that the parties involved, while operating under a process of 'recognition', do not fundamentally recognise each other. That is, the differend presumes a condition of incommensurability, of mutual misunderstanding, where the one can never hope to comprehend the other's point of view even as they may very well live together in the same place. Now this is obviously a seductive and often even necessary position to occupy within the frame of postcolonial politics. Many Aboriginal claims for sacredness depend on stressing the fact that their view of the land is entirely different to, and distinct from, 'ours'—and that 'we' can never hope to understand it (a position which is quite different to David Tacey's, which had suggested not only that we can understand these things, but that we can then absorb and transcend them, too!). This position is also often supported by non-Aboriginal deliberations, most famously in Labor Prime Minister Bob Hawke's remark on the Jawoyn people's claim for the sacredness of Coronation Hill, that 'they are outside of an intellectual framework with which most of us are comfortable'.[38] So this is an available response to the sacred in Australia which can have a positive outcome, for Aboriginal people at least. But in our view, this can also generate a nostalgia for the sacred which allows it to proceed into the modern nation only as the kind of residue we had remarked upon at the beginning of this chapter. Now this is not to say that through this process the sacred is deactivated entirely. In fact, the 'residual', for Raymond Williams, is distinguished from the 'archaic' precisely because the former 'is still active in the cultural process'.[39] Nevertheless, this view of the sacred withdraws it from modernity through claims which depend upon stressing its incommensurable difference; and this can work paradoxically as a form of restraint. Under this logic, the sacred is not allowed to speak about itself. And this withdrawal, this silence, carries with it losses, as well as gains.

In his description of Lyotard's concept of the differend, Bill Readings focuses on a film which actually attempts to stage the incommensurable dispute between Aboriginal people and mining companies in Australia: Werner Herzog's *Where the Green Ants Dream* (1984). For Readings, this film provides a perfect example of the differend as it functions in a postcolonial nation, and we shall quote his account of it at length:

> The mining company has one kind of claim ('legal title', deeds, etc.). The aborigines (*sic*) have another kind of claim (sacred buried objects). There is not simply a dispute as to who owns the land; the notion of 'property' as such is the locus of a differend. The film stages this in two exemplary double binds. The aborigines are asked to substantiate their claim by producing the sacred buried objects as if they were 'evidence' for the court. They reply that they cannot do this, because to look at the sacred objects would be a sin, resulting in the death of the viewer. Second, an aborigine hitherto known as 'The Mute' stands up the court and suddenly begins speaking. The judge asks why he is called 'Mute' if he can speak, and demands a translation. The other aborigines reply that he is called 'Mute' because the rest of his tribe are dead; no one else speaks his language, and he speaks no other. The judge expresses sympathy for the aborigines but concludes that they have presented nothing to the court which is admissible as legal evidence. In each case, the aborigines are not litigants but victims: they have suffered a wrong, and the nature of that wrong removes the capacity to prove it before the law. No tribunal can resolve the case, either way, without victimizing one side or the other, rendering them 'Mute'. Any judgment that claims to have the last word on this case will necessarily victimise one side or the other, since [according to Lyotard] 'the rules by which one judges are not those of the judged genre or genres of discourse'.[40]

This film, made by a German director, no doubt presents an outsider's sympathies with Aboriginal claims for sacred land. But it does so by reproducing the process of restraint we had noted earlier.

An Aboriginal man speaks in court here, but he is not understood; he speaks 'in language' which no one can follow (including other Aboriginal people). We need hardly point out the unlikelihood of this actually happening under modern conditions: this is little more than a romantic fantasy about 'the last of a dying race'. Herzog simply gives us an image of Aboriginal people in court unable to sustain themselves; and he does this by locating them as a residue which is increasingly out of place in modernity. But Aboriginal people do sustain themselves in court, often with great success: the relationship between sacredness and modernity, far from being incommensurable, is continually under (re)negotiation. They are always in touch with each other: this is a highly promiscuous relationship! In Herzog's film, the Aboriginal sacred exists only in the form of a monologue; but in postcolonial Australia it is produced and reproduced through a process of dialogue. There is always someone to speak to, and there is always someone else to answer back.

So how can we express the way in which the Aboriginal sacred impacts upon modern Australia? How can we account for this promiscuity between the two? We know that sacredness can function as much more than just a 'mute' residue; indeed, its political effects can be far-reaching, luxurious and decidedly unsettling. Paradoxically, a minority politics, at precisely the moment at which it constitutes itself as a minority, may then insinuate itself into the broadest possible framework: all over the place. Of course, it is important to say here that to be in a 'minority' is not always to be oppositional: a modern nation may very well feel ambivalent about its minorities, sometimes enthralled by them (as New Age-ism has been), sometimes revulsed by them. Ambivalence, as we have already noted, is the most appropriate way of registering this predicament. As far as the Aboriginal sacred is concerned, non-Aboriginal people may well be sympathetic to it, even as they recognise the unsettlements it may cause (its often massive legal costs, its demands on land, its apparent disregard for capitalist interests and the welfare of the nation, its reminder that Aboriginal people have ongoing agendas). So what word can we use adequately to describe this ambivalence? The *differend* has its drawbacks; but another word, also connected to legal processes (which often determine the outcome of disputes over sacredness), might be invoked: 'solicit'. We should not apologise for the fact that this word appears almost incidentally in the work of another continental theorist, Jacques Derrida's famous essay 'Différance' (1970).

Here, Derrida alerts us to some of the meanings embedded in the kind of structure which involves one thing 'soliciting' another thing—when 'solicit' is taken as an activating verb. But let us give a fuller picture of this word's activating possibilities here. It can mean, firstly, 'to incite', 'to allure', 'to attract'—mostly by the use of gentle force. Now obviously, this evokes a feminised image of the sacred, although it is worth noting that 'soliciting' is not the prerogative of one particular sex. As with Durkheim, this imaging of the sacred admits the possibility that modernity can be attracted to it, even intimate with it; but unlike Durkheim, it gives the sacred a much more unsettling function in return. Other meanings embedded in the word 'solicit' elaborate this latter function: it also means, 'to disturb', 'to make anxious', 'to fill with concern'. Professor Burton's lament, 'What am I going to tell my students in the future?' amply gives expression to this effect of the sacred. But there is a further meaning tied up with the word 'solicit', which Derrida's translator remarks upon and which we also should mention: 'to shake the whole, to make something tremble in its entirety'.[41] Let us note the possibility here that sacredness—a claim for an Aboriginal sacred site, for example—can 'shake' the entire nation, a possibility we shall return to during the course of this book. Hugh Morgan's response to the decision over Coronation Hill (that it was a 'shocking defeat' along the lines of the fall of Singapore) is, therefore, simply one particularly cataclysmic reading of the force of the sacred in modern Australia. One could equally as well read this force in a positive way, of course, as a way of inducing a productive realignment of power in an emergent postcolonial nation. In this context, we should remember the more obvious meaning of the word 'solicit': 'to conduct (a lawsuit)', 'to press or represent a matter', 'to transact or negotiate'. If we think of it in this way, the Aboriginal sacred, far from being restrained and 'mute', far from having nothing to say to modernity, becomes activated and dialogic. It is always in a position of negotiation, and this includes the negotiation of its own position in the framework of modernity.

It is time to make the argument of this book clear. By viewing the Aboriginal sacred as an activated thing, religiously, politically and discursively, we can begin properly to understand the means by which it continues to impact upon modernity. There could well be a certain level of incommensurability at stake here in the sense that Aboriginal sacredness may never be wholly understood; but nevertheless, it actively 'solicits' the modern nation in public forums too, producing comment and counter-comment, reaction and counter-reaction. In the process, this otherwise marginal thing accumulates such profound significance that it can effect, even reshape, the sensibility of the nation. But the transaction is not simply one-way. We also need to admit that modernity works to reshape sacredness in turn—restraining or regulating it in certain ways, unleashing it in others, reformulating the context in which it manifests itself. The impulse is, accordingly, towards reconciliation at one moment, and division at another: 'one nation' and a 'divided nation'. It is the ceaseless movement back and forth between these two positions which is precisely postcolonial. And the various promiscuities arising from this movement, where sacredness and modernity solicit each other, produce a condition for the nation which we will designate as 'uncanny'.

2

The Postcolonial Uncanny

On Reconciliation, (Dis)Possession
and Ghost Stories

I T IS TIME to introduce the concept of the 'uncanny' and to say
something about its value in relation to postcolonial Australia.
This concept comes into modern thinking through Sigmund
Freud's influential essay, 'The "Uncanny"', an essay published in
1919, four years after Durkheim's *The Elementary Forms of the
Religious Life*. Freud's primary concern is certainly with the psyche,
but the essay is also about one's sense of place in a modern, chang-
ing environment, and it attends to anxieties which are symptomatic
of an ongoing process of realignment in the post-war modern
world. In brief, Freud elaborates the 'uncanny' by way of two
German words whose meanings, which at first seem diametrically
opposed, in fact circulate through each other. These two words are:
heimlich, which Freud glosses as 'home', a familiar or accessible
place; and *unheimlich*, which is unfamiliar, strange, inaccessible,
unhomely.[1] An 'uncanny' experience may occur when one's home is
rendered, somehow and in some sense, unfamiliar; one has the
experience, in other words, of being in place and 'out of place'
simultaneously. This simultaneity is important to stress since, in
Freud's terms, it is not simply the unfamiliar in itself which generates the anxiety of the uncanny; it is specifically the combination of
the familiar and the unfamiliar—the way the one seems always to
inhabit the other. In postcolonial Australia, and in particular after
the *Mabo* decision in 1992, Freud's 'uncanny' might well be applied
directly to those emergent (that is, yet-to-be established) procedures
for determining rights over land. In this moment of decolonisation,
what is 'ours' is also potentially, or even always already, 'theirs': the
one is becoming the other, the familiar is becoming strange.

The value of this concept, then, is that it refuses the usual binary structure upon which much commentary on Aboriginal and non-Aboriginal relations is based. We often speak of Australia as a 'settler' nation, but the 'uncanny' can remind us that a condition of unsettledness folds into this taken-for-granted mode of occupation. We often imagine a (future) condition of 'reconciliation', and indeed, a great deal has been invested in the packaging of this image as a means of selling it to the nation—but the 'uncanny' can remind us of just how irreconcilable this image is with itself. It is not simply that Australians will either be reconciled with each other or they will not; rather, these two possibilities (reconciliation; the impossibility of reconciliation) coexist and flow through each other in what is often, in our view at least, a productively unstable dynamic.

There is another, not unrelated, binary structure at work in contemporary Australia which we can also comment on. In relation to Aboriginal people, non-Aboriginal Australians can either be innocent—in the sense of not being implicated in earlier processes of colonisation, or guilty—in the sense that everyone ('all of us') is drawn into 'the guilt industry' whether they like it or not. Paradoxically, the former position casts non-Aboriginal Australians as 'out of place', uninvolved in those formative colonial processes; while the latter position would conceive of non-Aboriginal Australians as, in fact, too involved, too embedded in place, in the sense that every one of them, even the most recent immigrant, automatically inherits the (mis)fortunes of Australia's colonial past. In postcolonial Australia, however, it may well be that both of these positions are inhabited at the same time: one is innocent ('out of place') and guilty ('in place') simultaneously. And this is entirely consistent with postcoloniality as a contemporary moment, where one remains within the structures of colonialism even as one is somehow located beyond them or 'after' them.

The topic of sacredness-in-the-midst-of-modernity can help to give the Freudian concept of the uncanny a certain concreteness in the context of modern Australia. Certainly, the Aboriginal sacred can retain a level of 'strangeness' and unknowability. These characteristics are produced by Aboriginal people when they speak about the sacred as a secret thing. But the production of the sacred as a secret necessarily unfolds in a modern framework, and this framework always carries with it a level of publicity, as we will show in many of the chapters to follow. One always says to someone else that the sacred is a secret. Its secrecy is always a matter of demonstration or performance. So in the case of the Aboriginal sacred, a dialogic relation is constructed between secrecy and publicity: they relate to each other through a process of soliciting, which is to say, they enjoy each other's company but they are also intensely wary of each other. The fortunes of the sacred at the moment are such that secrecy is always entangled with publicity to the extent that in modernity—for example, in the context of Aboriginal claims to land—they actually require each other to function, attracting and repelling each other in various ways. The dynamic which places them in relation to each other works by bringing them together then drawing them apart, and so on. This is a feature of the sacred-in-the-midst-of-modernity, which has secrecy and publicity compromise each other in order to produce the processes through which they continue to be identified as autonomous and intact. After all, secrets cannot be secrets until they are spoken about as such.

Let us imagine a structure where the Aboriginal sacred and modernity exist in such a dynamic relationship to each other. Now if the Aboriginal sacred was a passive and vulnerable thing, as Durkheim tended to suggest, then it would have a negligible effect on modernity's familiarity with itself. But if it is an activating, soliciting thing, and if it is not just in one place but potentially all over the place—or at the very least, if its location, its destinations and its outcomes are difficult to predict—then modernity experiences the kind of 'unfamiliar familiarity' with itself that the uncanny precisely describes.

This 'unfamiliar familiarity', this 'unsettled settledness', is, of course, by no means specific to contemporary Australia. Certainly it is modulated here in specific, interesting ways which we shall examine through this book; but it is also a condition which is experienced only too often elsewhere in the modern world. When a nation engages with others—indigenous people, immigrants, separatists—a sense of national identity is both enabled and disabled. The presence of 'foreigners at home' can intensify a nation's investment in the idea of a national 'self' at the very moment at which such an idea is traumatically unsettled. Julia Kristeva's book, *Strangers to Ourselves* (1991), is a meditation on this problematic which draws, inevitably perhaps, on the uncanny. A nation's engagement with 'foreigners' leads her to offer a definitive structure for modernity built around the tension between union and separation (what in Australia would be 'reconciliation', and the impossibility of reconciliation).[2] The problematic she proposes involves the fact that boundaries which might have distinguished the one from the other are no longer tenable or even recognisable. For Kristeva, a certain anxiety results which stems from the difficulty of disentangling what is one's 'home' from what is not one's 'home'—what is 'foreign' or strange. As Kristeva notes, Freud's uncanny speaks to this anxiety directly:

> Freud wanted to demonstrate at the outset, on the basis of a semantic study of the German adjective *heimlich* and its antonym *unheimlich*, that a negative meaning close to that of the antonym is already tied to the positive term *heimlich*, 'friendlily (*sic*) comfortable', which would also signify 'concealed, kept from sight', 'deceitful and malicious', 'behind someone's back'. Thus, in the very word *heimlich*, the familiar and intimate are reversed into their opposites, brought together with the contrary meaning of 'uncanny strangeness' harbored in *unheimlich*.[3]

In fact, 'unheimlich' is further glossed by Freud as meaning 'withdrawn from knowledge', obscure and inaccessible, as well as untrustworthy.[4] We might note that these have been available characterisations of Aboriginal relations to the sacred where, as we know, secrecy is often associated (by mining companies, by government officials, etc.) with deception. But even a racist charge of deception is open to the uncanny effect since it is spoken in a structure which can never be subjected to any definitive kind of verification. If Aboriginal people say that a sacred site is here, and a non-Aboriginal 'expert' says that this sacred site is somewhere else—which is the way some site disputes fall out—what you actually get is two sacred sites for the price of one! The latter claim, in other words, by no means disproves the former, nor can it ever hope to do so in any finalised way. It is not that there is no means of settling the dispute (which would amount to invoking the irreconcilable incommensurability of the differend); it is rather that the conditions of verification remain problematic, so that even after the dispute is settled a certain 'unsettledness' remains.

In this context, it is worth recalling that Freud himself had noted: '*heimlich* is a word the meaning of which develops in the direction of ambivalence'.[5] Kristeva's strategy is to internalise and individuate this ambivalence as a means of coping with it. We should, she suggests, come to terms with the 'stranger in ourselves': 'The foreigner is within us. And when we flee from our struggle against the foreigner, we are fighting our unconscious—that "improper" facet of our impossible "own and proper"'.[6] So Kristeva draws a connection between a 'foreigner' and the 'improper' unconscious which solicits one's sense of a 'proper' self, that is, one's sense of property, of being properly 'in place'. It would be worth noting, however, that her advocacy of a psychic coming-to-terms with the 'foreigner' within us all is itself a 'reconciliatory' gesture which would remove the kinds of ambivalence that adhere to the uncanny. But there is no need to wish 'improper' anxieties away, at least in the postcolonial context, where they may well have productive effects.

Australia could also have been a 'foreigner at home'. At least, this is the account given by Ross Gibson in his book, *South of the West: Postcolonialism and the Narrative Construction of Australia* (1992). For Gibson, Australia has been 'a duplicitous object' for the western world in the sense that it is both 'demonstrably a "European" society' (familiar) and yet also 'fantastic and other-worldly' (unfamiliar):

> Westerners can recognize themselves there at the same time as they encounter an alluringly exotic and perverse entity, the phantasm called Australia. Westerners can look South and feel 'at home', but, because the region has also served as a projective screen for

European aspiration and anxiety, Australia also calls into question the assumptions and satisfactions by which any society or individual feels at home.[7]

The sense of this last sentence is not quite clear, at least to us; but overall, Gibson seems to be saying that—from the externalised position of the westerner—one can imagine being 'in place' in Australia only through the realisation that one is also 'out of place'. Gibson, in fact, invokes the uncanny in his description (although it is an unacknowledged invocation): Australia is 'both strange and familiar, in other words, an enigma'.[8] Yet although it is prepared to indulge this image of Australia as an 'enigma' to the rest of the world, when his book looks at Australia from within it figures it in a way which seems to do away with the uncanny altogether.

Gibson is usually sceptical about the mythical teleology of 'settler' Australia, which fantasises about 'reconciliation' or (using Kristeva's word) union—where a colony 'would gradually "belong", it would eventually be "in place", and it would cease to be a colony'.[9] Yet from time to time he yearns for this teleology himself, especially, as it happens, when he is drawn to consider modern Australian landscape poetry. This is a literary genre which often works to produce a sense that settler Australians can be reconciled properly with place: think, for example, of the poetry (but not necessarily the politics) of Les A. Murray. Gibson reads landscape poetry as a way of securing an authentic relationship to place, but he does this only by dividing it from 'the acquisitive process' that relationship might (in another reading) have depended upon: 'It is the development of this sense of subjective immersion in place, this ability to place and to think oneself in systems of settlement other than the acquisitive process of conquistadorial survey, that might be a reason for optimism as the third colonial century commences in the South Land'.[10]

So it is as if the 'immersions' of landscape poetry can neutralise 'conquistadorial' practices. And this allows Gibson to concoct the optimistic possibility of being 'at home' in Australia at last—a possibility he had queried elsewhere in his book. His homely space, however, is not entirely bereft of otherness:

But this is not to say that everyone has redefined their understanding of their place in the landscape. The more militarist attitude, which sees the continent as a foe to be brought to rule, still ranges abroad. The submerged domes of Pine Gap are obvious talismans: white Australians' (mythically induced) sense of the untouchability of the geographical centre has been turned to military advantage: what better place to locate unknowable technology than the arcane heartland where Nature preserve the most occult of mysteries? It is a canny [that is, not uncanny!] ploy. Whereas white Australia has traditionally looked for security *from* the landscape, a black magic promises to turn the world upside down by maintaining that there is security *in* the landscape . . . When the land becomes so otherworldly that only a 'masonic' class of technocrats can administer it, the conquistadorial class has taken its project to its end point . . .[11]

This is a passage which speaks directly against acquisition: technocrats against the homeliness of landscape poets. But how is the otherness of the 'conquistadorial class' figured here? Uncannily, Gibson figures it through an image of a sacred site. We are directed to 'the submerged domes of Pine Gap' at the 'geographical centre' of Australia, rather than, say, to Uluru. This installation is made 'otherworldly'; it is secretive, 'masonic'; it uses (in a bizarre slippage into 'primitivism') 'black magic'; it unsettles Gibson's yearning for homeliness-in-the-nation. We can note that this particular 'sacred site' is indeed a modern one! And, in fact, it is modernity itself which produces the uncanny effect for Gibson's ideal of settlement—a modernity which is uncomfortably underwritten by globalised, 'militarist' capital. Indeed, what we have with Gibson's image of Pine Gap is a textbook case of the uncanny effect: through an act of repression, Pine Gap appears unfamiliar to Gibson precisely because it provides him with an image of modernity which is all too familiar. So Pine Gap is to Gibson what (in his account) Australia is to the rest of the world: 'Both strange and familiar, in other words, an enigma'. Of course, if, under modernity, Australia were able to be settled through any form other than capitalism, then it might truly *be* an enigma. By imagining an Australia divorced from globalised capital, Gibson gives us a nostalgic structure where one can be 'subjectively immersed' in the former in order to remain alienated from the latter. In this arrangement, it would not be Australia that is an 'enigma' to the west, but the other way around.

When Julia Kristeva thinks about one's relations to the 'foreign', she wonders what kind of response might be forthcoming: 'To worry or to smile, such is the choice when we are assailed by the strange; our decision depends on how familiar we are with our own ghosts'.[12] We might well ask, how familiar is Australia with its own ghosts? Who 'smiles' at them and who 'worries' about them? This is a question of particular relevance to a nation which is involved, as Australia is, in an officially sanctioned process of reconciliation. Reconciliation is a policy which intends to bring the nation into contact with the ghosts of its past, restructuring the nation's sense of itself by returning the grim truth of colonisation to the story of Australia's being-in-the-world. But it is not surprising that, rather than laying things to rest, these ghosts (and the past is always ghostly here) in fact set a whole range of things into motion: arguments over land, debates over the 'proper' history for Australia, the bother about compensation and saying 'sorry' (and whether these things would settle the past down, or whether they would unleash it to the extent that the sayer—think of Prime Minister John Howard here—feels he would be subjected to a multitude of claims from which the country may never recover).

Let us turn, then, to a genre of writing—the Australian ghost story—which confronts these issues directly, tuning into the landscape in a very different way from the kind of poetry which Ross Gibson had privileged. It would seem that the ghost story in Australia is a minor genre, a marginal genre. To recall Durkheim's telling phrase, the ghost story is 'rudimentary' (an 'elementary' form, something less than literature), and yet there is also something 'gross' or luxurious about it, too. These contradictory characteristics are built into the sensationalism of this genre. Many Australian ghost stories are 'over-the-top', hysterical, histrionic, spectacular, overflowing, meandering, 'creaky', indulgent: all this takes place under the constraints of a minor genre.

The haunted sites of ghost stories may appear empty or un-inhabited—but they are always more than what they appear to be. These are 'excessive' things, extending both downwards (you will sooner or later uncover a ghost), and outwards: vertically and horizontally. Australian ghost stories generally do not respect the 'localness' of their sites; they are by no means constrained in this sense. Instead, they show how their sites work to influence or impress people who are always passing through, people who take the effects of those sites elsewhere when they leave (as they usually do), spreading them across the nation. The Australian ghost story, then, works by dramatically extending the influence or reach of its haunted site. It produces a site-based impression which spirals out of itself to affect others elsewhere, perhaps influencing even a nation's sense of its own well-being. So a supposedly 'marginal' thing can account for far more than its marginality would suggest.

Australia has a ghost of its own, of course: the bunyip. There have been a number of stories, usually by non-Aboriginal writers, which have located the bunyip in swamps or waterholes and represented the creature as frightening, often foreboding death—as in Rosa Campbell Praed's 'The Bunyip' (1891). Praed's story, which can be designated as 'late colonial', gives us a creature who is heard rather than seen: this particular ghost only signifies itself aurally, as a sound. The sound works to both spread this haunted site and to confuse its origins: 'Though we tried to move in the direction of the voice, it was impossible to determine whence it came, so misleading and fitful and will-o'-wisp-like was the sound'.[13] The haunted site in this story, then, is all over the place. There is no explanation for the bunyip: it has no origins. Praed is simply concerned with the effect this creature has on those settlers who pass through the bush. As she so beautifully puts it in her story, in a way that exactly recalls Kristeva's 'smiles' and 'worries', the bunyip 'deals out promiscu-ously benefits and calamities from the same hand'.[14] Let us just pause over this adverb 'promiscuously' for a moment. It returns us to that sense, already suggested by our consideration of the term 'solicit' in the context of sacredness in Chapter 1, that the haunted site, at least potentially, is an unbounded or luxurious thing which can reach across place indiscriminately. Praed's bunyip gives expression to these features, for there is no sense that one can refuse it; the thing takes effect and draws you in, for better or worse, whether you want it to or not.

These early settlers in Praed's story (which seems to be set some time before the 1890s) are yet to become 'homely', for they have been following a 'dray, loaded with stores and furniture for the new home to which we were bound'.[15] In other words, these settlers are still unsettled, and their talk about 'eerie things' speaks directly to that condition. In a certain sense, they contribute to their haunting and their own unsettlement, since the bunyip is animated only when they talk it up ('as we talked a sort of chill seemed to creep over us').[16] The creature 'promiscuously' emanates its aura through the bush, touching the settlers, preoccupying them and forestalling their homely impulses. Far from being 'subjectively immersed' in the landscape these settlers are, at least for the moment, out of place or displaced. The bunyip becomes a figure for displacement, in effect, and in this sense it has a postcolonial function.

Ghost stories are traditionally about possession; one takes possession of a haunted house and is possessed in return; all this happens on a property which is usually imagined as malevolent and overwhelming. Praed's late colonial story is about the moment before possession, before settlement, returning to that earlier moment to anticipate the 'improperness' of settlement even before it begins. Her characters, in other words, experience a moment of pre-occupation. But the postcolonial ghost story speaks not so much about possession as (dis)possession, coming as it does *after* the fact of settlement. It deals with post-occupational matters, which may fall out even more indiscriminately than in Praed's story. In this context, possession is there to be negotiated by different parties, settlers and Aboriginal people alike, whereas in the traditional ghost story there is no negotiation. Indeed, in Praed's story there is no one actually to negotiate with: there are no Aboriginal people attached to the haunted site (even though the bunyip may itself signify something 'Ab-original'). But in the postcolonial ghost story Aboriginal people return to the scene and, accordingly, are just as liable to be subject to hauntings as anyone else.

These features can be examined through a more recent ghost story told by an Aboriginal man to the well-known anthologist and poet, Roland Robinson. In the first part of Percy Mumbulla's narrative, also titled 'The Bunyip' (1958), this creature—which in Praed's story had been simultaneously 'promiscuous' and evasive— now appears to be monogamous and attached. The bunyip belongs to a 'clever old-man', an Aboriginal elder. It is known or familiar rather than unknown, and it is empowering rather than unsettling. Mumbulla's narrative suggests that the Aboriginal clever old-man derives his power directly from his bunyip:

> This old fellow had a bunyip. It was his power, his *moodjingarl*. This bunyip was high in the front and low at the back like a hyena, like a lion. It had a terrible big bull-head and it was milk-white. This bunyip could go down into the ground and take the old man with him. They could travel under the ground. They could come out anywhere. They could come out of that old tree over there.[17]

The Aboriginal clever old-man and the bunyip travel together with outcomes which are already difficult to predict. It is again not an issue of causes, so much as a question of destination: there is no telling where the old man and his bunyip will end up. The description of this bunyip is worth noting and aspects of it are repeated later on: 'That's when I saw the bunyip. He was milk-white. He had a terrible big bull-head, a queer-looking thing'.[18] The creature here is both exotic ('like a hyena, like a lion', 'queer-looking') and local; it seems to be both imported and indigenous. It is obviously associated with cattle, which would have frequented waterholes where bunyips are found, with attention drawn to its 'milk-white' colour. In a certain sense, then, this bunyip is produced by colonisation. It is· literally postcolonial and embodies some of this moment's features, the whiteness, the cattlelike anatomy, the indiscriminate ability to turn up anywhere unannounced, and so on.

Later, the Aboriginal clever old-man argues with his sister, who was 'as clever as he was'. They magically cause each other's deaths through the resulting power struggle, at which point the bunyip detaches himself and continues on his travels. In the first part of the story, then, the bunyip was in a settled relationship to its Aboriginal host, albeit in the framework of an unsettled geography (mobility, unpredictable outcomes, etc.). It leaves only when that settled relationship breaks down through the mutually inflicted deaths of the old man and his sister, deaths which the bunyip seems helpless to prevent. In the second part of the story, the bunyip is unleashed and in the process takes on an even more active function. At one point, he arrives unannounced at Percy Mumbulla's family home:

> My old dad was smoking his pipe by the chimney. Mum heard the bunyip coming, roaring. The ground started to shake. He was coming closer. He came out of the ground underneath the tank-stand. Went over to the chimney and started rubbing himself against it. He started to get savage. He started to roar. Mum told Dad to go out and talk to him in the language, tell him to go away, that we were all right.
>
> Dad went out and spoke to him in the language. He talked to him: 'We are all right. No one doing any harm. You can go away' . . . Every time Dad spoke to him, he'd roar. My old-man was talking: 'Everything is all right. Don't get savage here'.[19]

The narrative shows how this second Aboriginal man is now obliged to negotiate with this creature, to calm him down. The bunyip needs to be told that no one is 'doing any harm' to this family, and that as a consequence his powers are not required. This Aboriginal family, in other words, does not want to play host to this bunyip, which now functions as an unwanted guest in the sense that (much like modern paternalistic bureaucracies, for example) its concern for the family is drastically misplaced. We might even say, out of place: this bunyip has an 'unhomely' effect on what is clearly a 'homely' (that is, domesticated) scene. This is shown in the story by having the bunyip appear to have become 'primitive'—a feature which in this context unsettles this Aboriginal couple, and they send it away. At the same time, as we have noted, the descriptions of this bunyip draw attention to the creature's modern characteristics: far from being 'primitive', it is quite literally an introduced or imported species.

A number of contradictions are thus mobilised in this story. The bunyip is a 'milk-white' thing that is metaphorically connected to cattle, those very creatures that signify the dispossession of Aboriginal people as cattle-based properties expanded across the country. And yet a creature which is so animated by colonisation is nevertheless, initially at least, shown to contribute to Aboriginal empowerment. Later on, however, the creature is unleashed, becoming wilder, more 'savage', producing not empowerment so much as unsettlement. This savagery affects not the white settlers, as the bunyip had in Praed's story, but Aboriginal people: the narrator's homely mother and father. In fact, as we have suggested, this bunyip now quite literally has an unhomely character: turning up unannounced at their homestead, roaring wildly, suggestively rubbing himself up against the chimney, and so on. The creature itself is highly unsettled, highly mobile, marauding, his whereabouts now even more difficult to predict than before: 'He travels around, up and down the coast . . . He's even been seen in Victoria, at Lake Tyers Mission'.[20] So the second part of this strange story unleashes the bunyip to produce unsettling effects, not on whites this time, but on Aboriginal people. This seems to be because it now signifies two contradictory things: the 'primitive', from which this modern, homely Aboriginal couple has dissociated itself; and the postcolonial which, precisely because it is a modern thing, shakes up (that is, solicits: the sexuality implicit in this word is evident in the bunyip rubbing himself up against the chimney) the Aboriginal couple's home under the pretext of concern and demands their attention. Of course, there is no essential contradiction here: the modern can indeed seem 'savage' enough, although this no doubt depends on who is looking at it. This couple are thus caught in the middle of this contradictory movement between the 'primitive' and the postcolonial. It unsettles them, certainly; but we should pay attention to the way in which this Aboriginal couple engage with the bunyip as a matter of course. If nothing else, the later part of this strange story shows these Aboriginal characters keeping their place, and their sense of place, through direct negotiation.

We have said that the Australian ghost story is a minor or marginal genre. Australian writers and film-makers have not yet spectacularised this kind of story, as the United States has, through big-budget movies such as *Poltergeist II: The Other Side* (1986), which is all about a settler family inhabiting a new house built upon an apparently empty site that turns out to be an Indian burial ground, a site which is reanimated in order to move the family on (but where to?). Nevertheless, there have been several quite recent and

significant interventions in the genre, two of which we would like
to discuss in some detail: Tracey Moffatt's *BeDevil* (1993), and
Margot Nash's *Vacant Possession* (1996). Both of these have been
prize-winning films: *BeDevil* won an award for best sound at the
Festival of Fantastic Cinema in Barcelona and was selected for Un
Certain Regard in the 1993 Cannes Film Festival; while *Vacant
Possession* won the Special Jury Prize at the 1996 Creteil Women's
Film Festival. They are both films about hauntings, and we use them
here mostly as points of contrast in our contemplation of the trou-
bled entanglements of possession and dispossession, settlement and
unsettlement.

Nash's film shows its non-Aboriginal protagonist, Tessa,
returning as an adult to her childhood home in Botany Bay, an
'original' place of Australian settlement. The film focuses on this
now dilapidated and abandoned family home and the traumas that
unfold when she returns there after her mother's death. People
ceaselessly pass through the house during Tessa's stay; it is an 'open'
place, full of visitors, ghosts and memories, some of them uninvited,
some of them calamitous. But the ghosts, in particular, are largely
self-made, stemming from Tessa's personal anxieties about the
unfinished business of the past. As an adolescent girl she had fallen
pregnant to an Aboriginal boy, Mitch, who had lived nearby. Her
racist father violently intervened in their affair, shooting and
wounding Mitch and driving Tessa away from the family home. The
film then works towards its climax during her return to the home
much later on as an older woman. Her father arrives unannounced,
rather like the bunyip in Mumbulla's story. There are other guests,
too: Millie, an Aboriginal girl from next door, and Tessa's sick white
cat, too obviously named 'Captain Cook'. Millie, Tessa and her
father sit down together for a meal. The traumatic histories of
nation and family are drawn together around the table, and the
consequences are nothing less than Gothic: a tempestuous storm
erupts to shake the very foundations of the family home in Botany
Bay. The unlikely trio (the cat remains upstairs) takes shelter in the
cellar, during which time father and daughter, Aboriginal and non-
Aboriginal neighbour, confront and lay to rest the ghosts of their
past. The house is blown away in the tempest, as if dispossession
must be shared equally in order for Tessa to achieve a 'proper'

homecoming. The cat, Captain Cook, dies during the storm and is later buried, signifying the successful transition into a suitably postcolonial sensibility.

Nash's film shows how Tessa becomes increasingly reconciled to the people and the place she left behind. Indeed, reconciliation is precisely what this film is all about: it speaks quite self-consciously to the national condition, using Tessa's homestead as an image of Australia itself. The ghosts of the past unsettle only in order (quite literally, since the characters are down in the cellar) to produce the kind of 'subjective immersion' that Ross Gibson had found in modern Australian landscape poetry, which then serves as the necessary prerequisite for reconciliation. Let us make this point clearer: reconciliation, as it is conceived in this film, rests on a non-Aboriginal character returning home in order to become *both immersed and dispossessed*: to become homely and homeless at the same time (a strange entanglement also charted in a recent book about the loss of one's home by the Australian historian, Peter Read).[21] That is, this non-Aboriginal character is reconciled by becoming 'Aboriginal' in a postcolonial sense: immersed in the landscape, but dispossessed of property: all in the frame of Botany Bay (un)settlement. Indeed, Tessa's Aboriginal neighbours provide the means by which this familial form of reconciliation occurs: they are facilitators in this respect, enabling the kind of individualised coming-to-terms Julia Kristeva had advocated in *Stranger to Ourselves*. The smooth, reassuring jazz music score keeps this theme intact: everyone finally gets on together, in this ultimately untroubled (the storm finally blows over) fantasy of homely cohabitation through a dispossession everyone can share.

Tracey Moffatt's *BeDevil* works somewhat differently. On the whole, this film—which presents three quite separate ghost stories—was reviewed in a perplexed way. According to Ronin Films' publicity flyer (wittingly or unwittingly) this is a film 'where the unexplained happens' rather than the unexpected, a comment which set the tone for *BeDevil*'s reception. In particular, it was seen to be indulgent and unnecessarily obscure. Unlike *Poltergeist II*, for example, these stories did not privilege the explanation of the hauntings; and unlike *Vacant Possession*, they did not even seem to offer a coherent narrative about the hauntings. It is worth noting that Moffatt, an Aboriginal film-maker, did not seem particularly interested in reanimating some kind of precolonial imaginary as Rosa Praed had done; nor did she return us to the site of colonial trauma to confront the past and lay the ghosts to rest. Indeed, the point about her film is that all the ghosts are modern and, far from being laid to rest, they continue to flourish under modern conditions.

The first story, called 'Mr Chuck', focuses on a swamp haunted by the ghost of a black American soldier from World War II. The second story, 'Choo Choo Choo Choo', refers back to the ghost of a young white girl killed on a railway track. The third story, 'Lovin' the Spin I'm In', shows a townscape haunted by a young Aboriginal couple who broke with traditional law in order to marry. In each of these stories there is again little interest in how the ghosts came to be where they are, or even in how they came to die. The interest is almost completely in the effects they have on those nearby or on those passing through. In the process, the issue of possession is never fully resolved: these are ghost stories which refuse the fantasy of a fully embodied reconciliation.

All three of the stories go on to show the 'modern-ness' of conditions which build up around these haunted sites. In 'Mr Chuck', a cinema is built upon the swamp which contains the body of the dead black American soldier. The bubbling swamp looks like it might well contain a bunyip, but the emphasis now is solely on the ghost's introduced qualities (the black American soldier does not belong; he was just visiting), not its indigenous qualities. We can very well see this cinema on a swamp as another version of Ross Gibson's militarist Pine Gap in that it certainly seems to activate an aberrant form of 'black magic' in the country! This cinematic story thus self-consciously puts cinema itself in the frame of modernity, and in the frame of 'elemental' effects which can be passed on (to the viewer). Cinema and ghosts are entangled together here, in other words; and for Moffatt in particular, who relies on noise and music and choreography rather than dialogue, film certainly does work as a highly affective (we might even say, recalling Durkheim again, a luxuriant or indulgent) form of media.

Moffatt's ghost story also looks at the ability of a haunted site to reach out far beyond its otherwise limited domain. At one point, as a means of closing a white woman's narrative of the events, the camera relocates itself to rise up into the air to present a number of wide-screen panoramic landscape shots showing 'settled' Australians at their leisure: at the beach, riding bicycles, playing cricket, and so on. The story thus overflows its boundaries, giving a view of the modern 'nation' at play—after which it then returns to the 'localness' of the haunted site and the cinema which has been built upon it. The movement away from the site and towards the 'nation' then back to the site again, works to implicate the one in the other. This is the uncanny effect of the ghost story, since it puts the haunted site into a 'familiar' location and in doing so it makes that location appear strange. This produces an equation for ghost stories which we can list as follows: the site is (not) the nation. The point would distinguish this film from Nash's *Vacant Possession*, which is all too ready to make Tessa's homestead a thing of national significance. Moffatt's film, on the other hand, suggests a resemblance and refuses to allow that resemblance to settle. There is a striking contrast between the introverted traumas of the haunted swamp and the innocent fun of Australians-at-their-leisure. Those Australians are allowed to go about their business in an unpreoccupied state of bliss. But let us draw attention to the musical sequence which accompanies the camera as it rises into the air. In contrast to the smooth, seamless jazz score which accompanies Nash's film the music here is sharp and shrill, and in the background, almost inaudible, are the sounds of chains being rattled and a man shouting: 'Get up!'. This is a rare moment in *BeDevil*, when there is actually an affective connection back to colonialism and colonial trauma, involving the forced clearing of Aboriginal people away from land that is now being enjoyed by these modern, leisured Australians. Obviously, it works to undercut the innocence and the familiarity of that panoramic sequence of non-Aboriginal settlers at play. But at the same time, it remains as a background feature of that sequence which you can very nearly not hear. The innocence of the sequence is almost preserved, but not quite. We can return to our earlier point about the enmeshing of innocence and guilt, since the sequence identifies postcolonial settlement through the mutuality of these positions: that the leisured or 'luxurious' activity of modern Australians is played out in a postcolonial field in which implication can be cast both ways (depending, of course, on one's 'position', on what one hears). The central character in this ghost story is an Aboriginal boy who is drawn to the cinema on the swamp. It seems at first as if he is attracted by the cinema alone, enthralled by its modern offerings. Indeed, cinema looks as if it functions as an image of modernity here. It signifies leisure and luxury, for example—it is full of confectionery, which the boy greedily devours—and it seems utterly oblivious to the ghost bubbling away beneath its surface. At the same time, the film brings the cinema and the ghost together: the modern always brushes against the elemental. The Aboriginal boy breaks into the cinema, climbing in through the window; soon afterwards, he falls through the wooden floor to touch the swamp with his foot, whereupon the ghost rises to lick him and spit at the camera (which is about as far as 'subjective immersion' takes us in this ghost story). So elemental forces rise in this film, but not to blow the building away as they had done in *Vacant Possession* in order then to produce a 'proper' mode of settlement. Rather, the building is solicited. Its boundaries are transgressed through a sequence of incursions which bring the Aboriginal boy and the ghost together through the very structure of a modern building. In this sense, 'Mr Chuck' is a story about inhabitation, as opposed to co-habitation. It does not require the cinema to be obliterated because it knows that modernity is always there, enthralling in its own way. But it does suggest that, even so, modernity is never fully in possession of itself. The story does not offer a fantasy of loss or dispossession in order for us all then to resemble each other; rather, it tells us that modernity is in a state of (dis)possession, never lost to itself but never properly secure either.

We have already mentioned one way in which the ghostly effects of the stories in *BeDevil* spread beyond themselves. Another way this happens is by having the stories told by many different characters: Aboriginal and non-Aboriginal, indigene and immigrant. The film seems to carry with it a multicultural agenda which demonstrates that knowledge about ghosts is mobile: it travels, like gossip. Narrators often talk about a haunted site from somewhere else, from a suburban home, for example. In 'Choo Choo Choo Choo', we only hear about the haunted railway siding after the

Aboriginal woman has travelled to another site with her friends. So the effects of the hauntings are spread, both across cultures and across place: the sites, in other words, spiral out of their location even as they remain where they are. This means that it becomes increasingly difficult to distinguish between those who pass by and those who get drawn in—between, once again, the innocent and the implicated.

We can see this feature most clearly in the last story, 'Lovin' the Spin I'm In'. It begins with two transnational property developers coming into town to negotiate a deal to turn a supposedly 'disused' and unoccupied warehouse into a casino—a familiar enough narrative in many of Australia's cities. But the warehouse is inhabited by Emelda, a Torres Strait Islander, and the ghosts of her dead son and his lover. Now Emelda and the two ghosts are already dispossessed: the lovers had, through their elopement, violated traditional law and were banished from their traditional land, and Emelda follows them. So the warehouse is both their place and not their place (since they are 'out of place'): in this sense, all three Torres Strait characters are already diasporic and modern. An equally diasporic group, a Greek migrant family, are Emelda's neighbours and landlords. The Greek mother narrates part of the story, and her narration helps to establish her son's later attraction to the warehouse—much like the Aboriginal boy's attraction to the cinema in 'Mr Chuck'. The warehouse, then, is a place of pre-occupation: it draws people in. The property developers arrive expecting the building to be demolished, but it remains standing and inhabited in a way which troubles the premise of vacant possession that their development plans depend upon. Emelda is finally driven out of the warehouse, but in her absence the ghosts of her son and his lover become restless. They entice the dreaming Greek boy into the building, enthralling him with the passion of their relationship. As the ghostly lovers dance the building appears to 'overheat'; the boy's father, Dimitri, is summoned out of his bed to investigate and at the moment of climax, the property speculators return, only to be frightened away by what they encounter.

Again, the building remains in this story: it is never demolished for the sake of a fantasy about reconciliation outside the frame of settlement. But the building remains in order to be solicited by conflicting desires. The story seems to entangle Aboriginal (dis)possession, the enthralment of the Greek boy's erotic waking dream and the disdainful acquisitive pragmatics of off-shore development interests. The uncanny effect here is that (dis)possession becomes the shared feature, not reconciliation. The flow of this effect is by no means one-way. Certainly, capital produces further, traumatic dispossessions (and in this story, Emelda is once again moved on); but the pre-occupied site unsettles the interests of capital in return. The final image of 'Lovin' the Spin I'm In' seems to reflect this, with the property developers frantically trying to flee the scene, their car spinning around on its axis always apparently about to leave but *still held by the force of the haunting.*

We have wanted to highlight the genre of the Australian ghost story because of its potential in relation to the uncanny and in relation to the fortunes of a modern, postcolonial nation. We can think of this genre in terms of an entangled kind of haunting, which gives expression to a sense of (dis)possession for both Aboriginal people and non-Aboriginal people alike. And yet that word 'alike' does not properly speak to the effects of this entanglement: it is not just a question of resemblance or sameness ('all of us'), just as it is not always a question of difference. 'Ghosts' simply could not function in a climate of sameness, in a country which fantasises about itself as 'one nation' or which imagines a utopian future of 'reconciliation' in which, as Nash's film would have it, all the ghosts have been laid to rest. But neither can they function in a climate of nothing but difference, where the one can never resemble the other, as in a 'divided' nation. A structure in which sameness and difference solicit each other, spilling over each other's boundaries only to return again to their respective places, moving back and forth in an unpredictable, even unruly manner—a structure in which sameness and difference embrace and refuse each other simultaneously: this is where the 'ghosts' which may cause us to 'smile' or to 'worry' continue to flourish.

The Sacred (in the) Nation

On Boundaries, Aboriginal Bureaucracy and the Arbitrariness of the Sign

THE ANTHROPOLOGIST Kenneth Maddock, in his article 'Metamorphosing the sacred in Australia' (1991), rightly observes that, far from being in decline, the Aboriginal sacred 'has been making a return' in contemporary Australia.[1] Maddock goes on to chart this return, beginning with early interventions by the Australian anthropologists Walter Baldwin Spencer and Frank Gillen who had influenced Durkheim, and who, Maddock says, 'were addicts of the sacred'.[2] For Maddock, Spencer and Gillen 'established an association between Aborigines and sacredness'; and he lists a series of phrases used by these anthropologists which included the word 'sacred': for example, 'the peculiar sacredness of the spot'.[3] The emphasis here is on sacredness as an exclusive thing, invested with prohibitions and confined to particular sites and objects. One comes to know about sacredness by knowing about those prohibitions, about what not to do and where not to go—sacredness is known negatively, in other words. Thus, the association between Aboriginal people and sacredness was conceived of anthropologically, for Maddock, in the somewhat pragmatic terms of its effects.[4]

In itself, of course, anthropology can recognise the sacred but cannot help to protect its perceived exclusivity from the threat of colonialism. (In fact, anthropology's addiction to the sacred is a functional part of that colonial threat, already breaking down exclusivity even as it offers it up as a definitive structure for sacredness.) In the case of sacred sites, the task of 'protecting' the exclusivity of the Aboriginal sacred fell to Australian law and governmentality, particularly through the development of State-

and Federal-based sacred sites authorities in the 1960s and 1970s. These authorities began the task of producing 'complete', often centralised, registers of such sites. That is, they produced a bureaucratised knowledge of the Aboriginal sacred where registration is required in order for it then to be 'managed'. These procedures for recognising Aboriginal sacred sites are a component in a broader planning system which has as its role the regulation of the many competing claims for use and possession of land (mining claims, heritage claims, pastoral claims, tourism claims and so on). But when the sacred enters a centralised regulatory system, it then becomes a national responsibility; law and governmentality work to amplify the sacred in this sense even as they locate it. In other words, at the moment of legal and governmental regulation, the sacred is deregulated. For example, its exclusivity is preserved (now also through the added weight of government prohibitions) but it is also compromised (since it has now entered a public domain, since it has become 'bureaucratic'). The 'peculiar sacredness of the spot' may now be clearly bounded, but it is also unbounded through the governmentally-driven construction of a larger system of sacredness which stretches across the nation.

For Maddock, the slippage of the sacred from anthropology to governmentality—although he does not exactly express it in this way—is symptomatic of the movement from colonialism to postcolonialism. Even as it attempts to settle the location of a sacred site, governmentality never manages to have the last word. As Maddock puts it: 'The story does not end there. If we look back we can see that the concept of a sacred site passed out of anthropological control once lawyers took it up. So, too, if we look around we can see that the concept is escaping from legal control'.[5] So Maddock gives the Aboriginal sacred an activated role, even in the midst of the powerfully regulating framework of government and the law. He is alert, in other words, to the powerful potential of the sacred under Durkheim's 'new conditions'. In fact, in his underrated but important book *Your Land is Our Land: Aboriginal Land Rights* (1983), he has a chapter which wonders exactly what limits can be placed on the modern sacred: 'All of Australia a sacred site?

This is not a facetious question'.[6] The problem here is that when sacredness is amplified like this, the value of its exclusivity is lost: it is no longer 'peculiar' to itself, although it certainly has the effect of making the *nation* seem 'peculiar'.

Maddock's main point in this chapter is that a sacred site, in modern Australia, has a certain 'indefinite' quality; it may not reach across the entire nation but it also is never simply a 'spot'.[7] A sacred site has a surrounding area which might also be considered 'significant'—but does 'significance' always amount to sacredness? Also, Maddock looks at how different States, at the time of writing, categorised sacredness in terms of different levels of transgression (focusing on desecration in some cases, unauthorised entry in others). Now, in this account of the fortunes of the modern sacred, it looks as if the role of governmentality is always privileged, that it functions as the motor of change with regard to sacredness (through regulation, amplification, etc.). But Maddock pauses for a moment to remark on Aboriginal engagements with these modernising structures: 'No culture is static, though what some observers call growth will be dismissed by others as degeneration'.[8] The mobility or adaptability of Aboriginal culture under modern conditions is always important to recognise. More importantly, though, it need not totally disenfranchise Aboriginal people from their sites, not least because of the amplification of sacredness *which has already taken place.*

In this framework, 'loss' (loss of traditions, loss of exclusivity) is only one possibility amongst others. As Maddock notes: 'places must also change in significance, whether by way of gain, loss or variation'.[9] In the past, most sacred site legislation has tended to assume cultural and locational stasis, as if Aboriginal people have had an uninterrupted relation to their sites even after colonisation. But for most Aboriginal people this has simply not been the case. So how do they speak about sacredness? To be 'elsewhere'—to be 'out of place'—does not of course rule out Aboriginal people knowing about sacred sites. But more to the point, in this modern context of the amplification of the sacred, one is never just 'dispossessed'. There is not a clear-cut equation between the fact of one's dispossession and the loss of sacredness; indeed, sacredness 'returns' to modern Australia in the *context* of dispossession. The uncanny feature of this is that dispossession and possession are not opposites of each other: in postcolonial Australia, one might rewrite this as '(dis)possession'. To be 'out of place', in other words, provides new ways of being 'in place', since the modern amplification of place (sites or 'spots') has made the distinction between these two conditions much less clear. Dispossession is not a passive condition by any means; within the frame of dispossession, renewed and even intensified modes of possession are produced. In the process, the exclusivity of the sacred (which renders it secret, unknowable, even unsayable) is potentially compromised—although this, too, may bring with it gains as well as losses.

Maddock ends his chapter on Aboriginal sacredness with a section titled, 'Why bother about sites?'. He presents two arguments for site protection: firstly, that the sites have value because of their intrinsic sacredness; and secondly, that they have value because they belong to Australia's heritage. The first argument rests on the 'localness' of the site, while the second rests on its relation to the nation's concept of itself. For Maddock, however, neither argument 'is conclusive': the former does not work because it cannot guarantee Aboriginal notions of sacredness will have precedence over other people's notions of what is of value, while the latter does not work because it takes sites out of their modern, activated context and turns them into relics from the past.[10] But these two positions on the sacred are by no means mutually exclusive: a sacred site can be intrinsically sacred as well as important to the nation's sense of itself. We have also wanted to suggest that the amplification of the sacred under the 'new conditions' of modernity works continually to defer the possibility of the sacred being nothing more than a relic. Maddock does end his chapter, however, by noting that governmentality does not have the last word on the sacred. The ossifying process of site registration, as Ronald Berndt had noted, can make a sacred site appear to be 'as "alien or almost-alien" to Aborigines as to other Australians'.[11] But Berndt's claim that a sacred site is estranged from its actual, lived context rests on a nostalgia for uninterrupted Aboriginal traditions. A very different kind of actual, lived context can build itself around the sacred, however, as Maddock notes: where these estranged sites are recovered 'as part of a self-conscious assertion of ethnic identity'.[12] In this arena of indigenous politics, a nostalgia for uninterrupted traditions is enacted in response to that estrangement—suggesting again that dispossession, as we have already noted, provides the very conditions for a renewed mode of possession to occur.

Maddock's subheading, 'Why bother about sites?' is, in part, answered in an account of the modern sacred given by Aboriginal site recordist, Ray Kelly, titled, as it happens, 'Why we bother'. Kelly works for the New South Wales National Parks and Wildlife Service. His account has two sections, one telling a story, and the other dealing with official site recording practices. This latter section focuses on the pedagogical and political potential of site recording: this is 'why we bother':

> It seems to me that many of the sites that we in the Sacred Sites team have recorded during the past five years will assist Aboriginal groups throughout New South Wales in their claims for land rights. The bora rings at Tweed Heads and at Tucki Tucki near Lismore will, I believe, be marvellous showpieces and tourist attractions. This will help Aborigines educate other Australians and visitors to Australia in the future.[13]

There seems to be no tension between the politicising of the sacred (to enable land claims) and the spectacularising of the sacred as a relic (for tourist display) in this account. Both of these effects are outcomes of a pedagogical interest in sacred sites. Of course, in the process the exclusivity of the sacred is (almost) done away with, as Kelly notes in relation to the Tweed Heads bora rings: 'It is a significant site, the sacred aspects of which have been lost. It can therefore be opened to the public'.[14] This point returns us to the question, when is a 'significant' site sacred or otherwise? In fact, the 'loss' of sacredness here corresponds to the formation of a much more directed structure of pedagogy which turns back to Aboriginal people. To open the site to 'the public' is not to alienate Aboriginal people from it; in fact, it works (or at least, it can work) to prevent their alienation:

To enable the Aborigines to become more familiar with their culture
and heritage, National Parks and Wildlife Service are intending to
hold five Aboriginal Relics Schools throughout the State of New
South Wales. These will give the Aborigines the unique opportunity
to learn more of their forefathers and to strengthen their identity. The
Service already has more than 9,000 sites on record . . . The New
South Wales Aboriginal Sacred Sites Survey has recorded the details
about some 380 sites of significance to Aboriginal people throughout
the State . . .[15]

Kelly produces an account here which connects the strengthening of
Aboriginal identity to the number of sacred sites under registration:
the more 'complete' the record is, the stronger Aboriginal identity
will be. In other words, a strong Aboriginal identity—which is
'familiar' with its place—is channelled through a modern process
of bureaucratisation. We need not imagine that bureaucratisation
governs the outcome of such an identity formation (it is never so
'complete'). Nevertheless, the latter is implicated in the former to a
considerable degree.

   This implication is given a certain uncanny kind of expression,
however, in the story Ray Kelly tells as an accompanying narrative.
It concerns a young Aboriginal man, Cooloombrah, who is about to
be initiated by his tribal elders. He is a character who 'learned
quickly and easily', becoming intimate with nearby sacred sites. The
problem for the elders is that he gains too much knowledge, too
soon. As Kelly tells it, this 'meant he became a nuisance to the func-
tioning of the social system. He was a reformer, I suppose'.[16] The
elders have a different perspective: they try, unsuccessfully, to have
Cooloombrah killed. So the story gives us an ambivalent view of
this younger, learned and much stronger Aboriginal man. He functions positively in relation to tribal traditions (later on, he saves the
tribe from annihilation), but he also functions negatively as a young
'nuisance' who knows too much (which unsettles the elders' authority). Can we take Cooloombrah as an image of the modern
Aboriginal site recordist, someone who 'reforms' the sacred by
taking it into new formations of knowing and learning, formations
with which his elders are not entirely comfortable? Kelly's account
of 'why we bother' thus gives us a character who 'bothers'

traditional structures of authority by knowing more than he should. This bothering produces gains and losses for his community: it means he is always viewed ambivalently. In the context of Kelly's second section—in which his involvement in the centralising registration of sacred sites is off-set by the intention to strengthen Aboriginal identity—we can identify the young upstart, Cooloombrah, in a highly particularised way: he is, in effect, an 'Aboriginal bureaucrat'. Stephen Muecke has noted elsewhere that this term (or image) carries a 'monstrous' contradiction with it, as if Aboriginal people somehow cannot be modern and 'Aboriginal' at the same time.[17] Certainly, Cooloombrah has a 'monstrous' function in Kelly's story, overreaching himself in a context which we can read as modern, and in this respect he compares very much with the attached-yet-free-ranging bunyip in Percy Mumbulla's story. So the bureaucratisation of Aboriginality—through procedures like site recording—is a modern process which, at the very least, is viewed ambivalently by structures of authority (Aboriginal in this case) which, at some time before this moment, had been more or less securely 'in place'.

It is sometimes noted that Aboriginal people have lost their authority over sacred sites precisely because they have become modern, as if to be modern is to eschew the traditional forms of authority one once had access to. An argument along these lines is touched upon by Stephen Muecke in his book *Textual Spaces: Aboriginality and Cultural Studies* (1992), which draws together much of Muecke's work with an Aboriginal elder from the Kimberley region in north-west Western Australia, Paddy Roe. Muecke's point is that traditional or premodern Aboriginal people—before they were dispossessed by colonialism—lived out a direct connection between language and place. Aboriginal people inscribed their language, their signifiers, directly on to their place, as if the one was as real as the other:

> we also have to be conscious of . . . the relation of 'knowing' to the form of inscription. It may be the case that terms like the Pitjantjatjara *tjukurpa* or the Nyigina *bugarregarra* mean all of the following: talk, marking, dream, dreaming site, dreaming track,

songline, sacred object, system of laws. These terms, as signifiers, may be thought of as not separate from the things they signify. In Aboriginal societies it may be the case that the signifier (that material part of the sign which is the physical trace; that is, sound or marking) is not thought of as abstractable from the signified (the 'other' part of the sign which is the 'meaning idea').[18]

In modern societies, however, the relationship between signifier and signified is by no means as coherent. It is, indeed, supposed to be arbitrary, a condition where meaning has become increasingly abstracted from what it is meant to refer to through what Muecke calls 'the pressure of particular uses'.[19] For Muecke, traditional, pre-modern Aboriginal languages 'never had to put up with the notion of the arbitrary signifier-signified relation';[20] but in modern societies, this notion would seem to be definitive. So what happens when Aboriginal people become modern or are touched by modernity? Muecke's arrangement of these relations would suggest that such an event can only be described in terms of loss—in particular, the loss of a mode of authorisation which relied on the security of that bond between language and place. Under modern conditions, this mode of authorisation can no longer be appealed to; the bond between language and place has been interrupted (much in the spirit of Percy Mumbulla's bunyip, who was once attached to an Aboriginal man but later breaks away). This amounts, of course, to saying nothing more than that modern Aboriginal people are dispossessed. But because the arbitrariness of the signifier-signified relation is taken as definitive of modernity (where the bond between language and place is no longer secure), dispossession becomes a shared characteristic across cultures. We are all dispossessed (in exile, out of place, etc.) in this sense: there is no difference between us.

The main problem with this arrangement is that it produces an association between authority and tradition that disenfranchises modern Aboriginal people; modernity itself is only seen negatively. Much of Muecke's work, as we have noted, is with an older Aboriginal man, Paddy Roe; and it is mostly directed towards saying how Roe's authority is constituted in language, as if Aboriginal authority, against the odds, remains largely intact under modern conditions. Muecke seems less comfortable with the work of younger Aboriginal people, however: he dismisses Sam Watson's novel *The Kadaitcha Sung* (1990), for example, as 'virtually unreadable'.[21] In this account, the modern Aboriginal novelist is paradoxically more 'othered', less familiar, than the traditional Aboriginal elder. So the entry into modernity is constituted here as a loss. We shall return to Muecke's work with Paddy Roe later on in this book; but for the moment, we could suggest that his implied connection between tradition, authority and possession on the one hand, and 'modern-ness', the loss of authority and dispossession on the other, sets up a structure that simply does not speak to the modes of empowerment many modern Aboriginal people are actually experiencing. Aboriginal dispossession is a reality, certainly; but as we hope our discussion of Kenneth Maddock and Ray Kelly has shown, there is no need to equate dispossession so completely with disempowerment. Indeed, new forms of Aboriginal authority may come into being through the very structures of dispossession—precisely because the relations between language and place are now so unbounded. Let us return to the uncanny here, and say again that one can never totally polarise these features (the traditional and the modern, authorisation and the loss of authority, etc.). The amplification of the sacred in the context of modernity—which occurs because of 'the pressure of particular uses', to recall Muecke's terms—means that to be 'out of place' is still to be 'in place'; to lose is also to gain. And indeed, for many non-Aboriginal people, as we have noted, Aboriginal people are seen to have gained *too much*. In particular, Aboriginal claims on land and sacred sites appear to some non-Aboriginal people to gain their power from nothing less than a perceived 'arbitrary' relationship between language and place—where to be modern and unbounded is to be more activated than ever before.

We should comment here that a slippage has occurred in our discussion, between the Aboriginal claim for sites which are understood as sacred (and often secret) and more general claims for territory. There is no doubt that Aboriginal land claims often acquire an inviolable force through recourse to the presence of sacred sites. Although not necessarily one and the same, Aboriginal territorial claims are often presumed to be claims for sacredness. The perception that territorial claims fold into the inviolability of sacredness produces a particular anxiety for some sections of non-Aboriginal Australia. Nowadays, almost all expressions of Aboriginal territory are bound up with expressions of sacredness: the former bears a synecdochal relation to the latter. Under a colonial framework, a claim for sacredness might have been relegated to the sphere of (for non-Aboriginal people, an unbelievable) spiritual belief which bore no apparent connection to property rights: to believe in a sacred site was not necessarily to own it. But in modern Australia this kind of relegation struggles to realise itself. And this is because, for reasons we shall elaborate later on, the connection between sacredness and territoriality is now only too apparent—where, because ownership and spiritual belief can no longer be disentangled, territorial claims have both manageable and unmanageable ('hard-to-believe') features.

Few organisations in the early 1990s were more zealous in their representation of a nation increasingly possessed by (dispossessed) Aboriginal people than the Australian Mining Industry Council (AMIC), now renamed as the Minerals Council of Australia. This is a professional body based in Canberra, which serves the interests of mining companies by lobbying the government, producing documents for 'public information', financing large-scale surveys, issuing media statements, sponsoring public speakers and so on. In June 1990 AMIC published an information leaflet titled *Shrinking Australia: Australia's Economic Future: Access to Land*. AMIC was bothered by the fact that 'about 26 per cent of the land surface of Australia is difficult to access', either because this land has been given over to conservation (for example, a national park), or is now under Aboriginal title. The point for AMIC was that such claims on land were proliferating: 'This is an 11 per cent increase over the 23.5 per cent figure determined by AMIC in early 1988'. They went on to predict that if all proposed conservation designations and Aboriginal claims were realised then 'nearly half of Australia's land area will be severely restricted or prohibited to exploration and mining'.[22] For mining interests, then, Australia was 'shrinking'. They characterised these other forms of land use as 'restrictive' for them—even though such forms were not necessarily exclusive, as AMIC itself recognised.[23] What acknowledging these other land uses does mean, however, is that mining companies must 'bother' themselves with consultation, negotiation, compensation, and possibly rejection—a bothering which AMIC at this time seemed to read as one aspect of this mode of restriction. The anxiety expressed in this document, then, lay in the fact that Australia itself might be held hostage to environmental and Aboriginal desires to make it more exclusive than it previously had been. So Maddock's by no means 'facetious' question about whether the entirety of Australia can be a sacred site, that is, a site that could at least potentially exclude other activity, was given a certain realisation in 1990 through AMIC's view of their own 'shrinking' interests.[24]

The uncanny feature of this account was that AMIC thus appropriated, on behalf of mining interests, the language and the positioning of the dispossessed ('we are all dispossessed . . .'). It responded to a perceived amplification of Aboriginal interests by claiming that 'the mining industry is being discriminated against'[25] to produce a peculiar reversal of fortunes, whereby AMIC's constituency represented itself as facing much the same kind of threat from Aboriginal people that Aboriginal people had earlier experienced from colonisation! The notion of a 'shrinking' world is usually taken these days, of course, to indicate what commentators on postmodernity often describe as a time-space compression: where the globalised forces of capital and communication overcome what Geoffrey Blainey had once famously called 'the tyranny of distance'. What were once inaccessible places are now accessible through, say, telecommunications networks, and so on. In the AMIC document, however, 'shrinking' was used in exactly the opposite sense: what was once accessible now seemed to become much less accessible, because of local forces which were expanding to overcome what may have been perceived as the tyranny of globalised mining companies.

AMIC's notion that Australia was 'shrinking' rested on at least three aspects. The first concerned territory, and saw Aboriginal people as engaged in a process of reterritorialisation which had no foreseeable end. That is, it saw Aboriginal people as expansionist—a view we shall return to in the next chapter—at the ongoing expense of mining interests. The second aspect saw the mining industry itself as 'shrinking', as endangered—which would have meant amongst other things, of course, that AMIC was losing its constituency. This was not only because there was supposedly less available land, but also because all mining activity was subjected to an increasing amount of costly governmental regulation which deterred investment and encouraged industry to move elsewhere, off-shore. We have already noted that governmental regulation can have deregulatory effects which cannot always be predicted. We can also note that governmental regulation is given a certain familiar identity, at least in this anonymous commentary on land rights from *Australia's Mining Monthly* (1992): 'The paternalism of Aboriginal bureaucracies . . . is what stops mining development in the Northern Territory'.[26] Here, the 'Aboriginal bureaucrat' featured once again as 'monstrous' (to recall Muecke's term), although now from the point of view of mining interests. Again, then, modern Aboriginal structures were seen to have an unsettling function and, in this case, produced a discourse that enabled AMIC to speak of itself without a trace of irony as 'discriminated against', endangered, dispossessed. We need hardly add that this is nothing less than an uncanny reversal of fantastic dimensions.

The third aspect of AMIC's notion of 'shrinking Australia' followed on from this: because the bond between mining interests and the fortunes of Australia as a nation was imagined to be so strong, the threat to the one was seen as a threat to the other. In 1991 Campbell Anderson, then vice-president of AMIC, remarked that the reterritorialisation of Australia by Aboriginal people created a 'sovereign risk'.[27] The interesting thing here is that mining interests, by choosing a discourse for themselves which diminished them in relation to Aboriginal expansion, actually helped to create this image of 'Aboriginal bureaucracies' laden with 'monstrous' levels of power; enough power, in fact, to 'restrict' mining interests and thereby solicit the nation that AMIC thought it had represented.[28]

In this account, then, AMIC implicated itself in the modern amplification of Aboriginal power. We should not imagine, of course, that AMIC and other mining interests were somehow naive about their own conditions; in fact, we have been struck by their commitment to theorisation and scholarship as a means of giving those conditions expression.[29] But it was something of a surprise to see Lauchlan McIntosh, AMIC's executive director at the time, actually working through the kind of uncanny amplification of minority politics that this book is, in part, concerned with. His 1987 article 'Land access and the shrinking world of mining' began with the kind of cataclysmic perspective on land access we noted in Chapter 1 in relation to Hugh Morgan:

> Despite the more readily apparent dangers to the Australian mining industry of weak commodity prices and shrinking markets, the most dangerous and most insidious foe the industry faces today is the creeping erosion of its right to explore for minerals and its right to mine those minerals it does find.[30]

He continued with a diatribe against the 'lunatic or radical fringe'— 'elite groups' who 'see the concepts of wilderness and heritage as backdoor ways to establish Federal legislation to protect an increasingly larger area of Australia from development'.[31] Soon afterwards, however, the nature of the 'fringe' is relocated:

> But it is not only some groups on the lunatic fringe which cause us worry. While the States would appear to have prime responsibility for environmental and conservation matters, the Federal Government has made itself a major player in the field—initially with the best of intentions, but eventually with the worst of consequences.[32]

Here it is governmentality which resembles the 'lunatic fringe', the latter being identified nationally and bureaucratically rather than simply with a 'radical' minority. This is a common enough strategy for business interests, of course; but then the nature of the 'lunatic fringe' is relocated a third time, somewhat surprisingly perhaps, back to the realm of mining interests:

> There is, of course, another lunatic or radical fringe. They are the explorationists or miners who continue to scar the landscape, who continue to build miles of unnecessary grid lines, drill sites, mining sites without regard for environmental planning and who leave behind a trail of destruction for which the whole mining industry is held accountable.[33]

For AMIC, then, the 'lunatic fringe' was apparently everywhere, even within its own ranks. Far from being relegated to the fringe, in other words, lunacy now seemed to be all over the place, even in the midst of the mining industry itself. McIntosh proposed 'self-regulation' as a solution, in line with AMIC's role as an overseer to the mining industry. There are two uncanny consequences of this proposal which, from our point of view, are worth commenting on. You cannot 'self-regulate' an industry whose 'self' is internally divided—where, as McIntosh observed in the remarks cited above, mining is already inhabited by a 'lunatic fringe' which continues 'to scar the landscape'. But more to the point, McIntosh's proposal of 'self-regulation' amounted to wanting the mining industry to come to resemble the very 'lunatic fringe' he had identified as opposed to mining in the first place. He concluded his commentary, in other words, by calling for the mining industry to be implicated in, even responsive to, the minority politics of environmentalism.

Mining interests at this time perceived the processes of regulation to be, in themselves, unstable: the 'risk' of mining is increased because the government, along with minority or 'single interests', continued to 'change the rules'.[34] AMIC was directly involved in the attempt to reintroduce some stability into this framework, notably through its sponsorship of a major mapping exercise designed to identify Aboriginal territorial limits. The results of this exercise were presented in S. L. Davis and J. R. V. Prescott's *Aboriginal Frontiers and Boundaries in Australia* (1992), and more recently, in S. L. Davis, Resource Managers Pty Ltd and the Australian Mining Industry Council's *Australia's Extant and Imputed Traditional Aboriginal Territories* (1993). Interestingly, in spite of the fact that AMIC funded a significant part of the research on which Davis and Prescott's book was based, these authors claim to offer a 'dispassionate analysis' of Aboriginal territoriality.[35] They invoke the objectivity of the scientist, in other words, as a way of transcending the partiality of a mining lobby group 'without whose assistance this information may not have reached the public domain' in the first place.[36] In fact, the objectivity of this project was compromised in other ways as well: for example, Aboriginal women were excluded from the research on the basis of an assumption that 'most information detailing and confirming the identities and distributions of territories seems to be held by men'.[37]

More broadly speaking, however, *Aboriginal Frontiers and Boundaries in Australia* reanimated a pragmatic form of geography which imprinted itself on the nation in nothing other than a belated way. Davis and Prescott's cartography was preceded some years ago by the seminal work of the anthropologist Norman Tindale, work which began in the 1920s and which produced his famous map of Aboriginal 'tribal' boundaries in Australia, published in 1940 and then published again in revised form in 1974. In their account of the early formation of Tindale's map, Davis and Prescott have this to say: 'Tindale worked on Groote Eylandt in 1921 and submitted his first paper showing exact boundaries in 1925. The editor, believing that Aborigines roamed at will over the whole country, refused to allow the boundaries to be shown as solid lines . . . They were shown as dotted lines!'[38] This expression of disbelief about boundary identification here gives us a useful insight into the shifting history of cartographic representations of 'Aboriginal Australia'. A colonial view (that of Tindale's editor) feels secure with an image of Aboriginal people as nomadic, as not bound to property, as 'naturally' dispossessed. But Tindale's map is a radical break with this perception, which is then compromised by those editorially imposed dotted lines which avow and disavow Aboriginal connections to place (property) simultaneously. When he finally came to produce his map of Aboriginal Australia in 1940 and again in 1974, Tindale was no longer editorially restricted to dotted lines and was able to spread this method of binding Aboriginal people to place right across the nation (Figure 1). In a certain, quite precise sense, this produced an 'unrecognisable' Australia: non-Aboriginal State boundaries are submerged by Aboriginal boundaries of place, and prominent non-Aboriginal landmarks (for example, cities such as Sydney or Melbourne) disappear under the weight and intensity of this remarkable record of Aboriginal occupation. With a map of Australia that is so bountiful, so complete, so full of Aboriginal territory, any cartographers who come along afterwards in the wake of Tindale—as Davis and Prescott do—can only leave their own mark by rubbing at least some of that fullness out.

So it is perhaps not surprising, then, that these two geographers speak often about loss in their book, notably, the loss of a particular kind of 'knowledge'. The problem for Davis and Prescott is that the

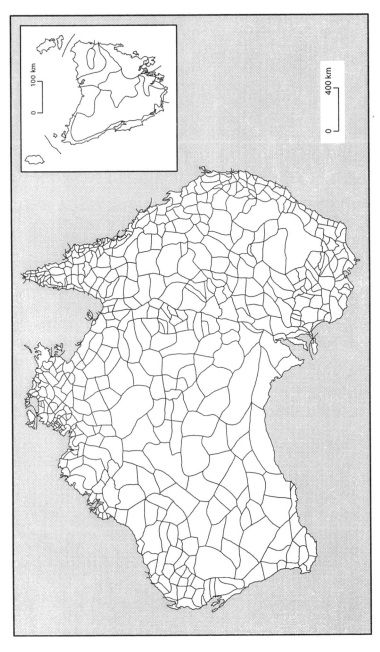

Figure 1 Tindale's map of Australia produced an unrecognisable nation so replete with Aboriginal territory that any cartographers who came along in his wake could only leave their mark by rubbing at least some of that repleteness out. (Adapted from Norman B. Tindale, *Aboriginal Tribes of Australia: Their Terrain, Environmental Controls, Distribution, Limits and Proper Names*, Canberra: Australian National University Press, 1974).

knowledge their research had privileged produces a map of 'Aboriginal Australia' which, in relation to Tindale's, is much diminished in its extent: 'The accumulation of this detailed knowledge will demonstrate that in large parts of Australia outside the tropics precise information about Aboriginal boundaries has been lost forever'.[39] The level of this diminution is given clear articulation in the national map later produced by Davis in conjunction with AMIC, where the north (the 'tropics') is densely covered with boundaries but the south—and especially the south-east—is 'empty'.[40] So whereas for Tindale Australia was fully inhabited by Aboriginal territory, these two geographers produce a binary in which 'fullness' (the 'tropics', the north) is contrasted with emptiness (the south). This binary works by equating the north with 'precise information' and the south with the loss of precision. That is, it equates the north with tradition, and the south with modernity:

> It seems to us that where the knowledge is intact land claims should be decided on the basis of that knowledge when proofs are provided. Where the knowledge about the precise extent of traditional territories has been lost mechanisms must be devised to make land grants or compensation without the charade of re-inventing knowledge or elaborating traditions that are imperfectly known or found in the records of anthropologists who did their work decades ago.[41]

This passage suggests that Davis and Prescott's research talked down knowledge about Aboriginal people which was seen to be already mediated, either through their suggestion of Aboriginal 'elaboration' or through earlier encounters with anthropology. They seem to prefer what they take to be an *unmediated* ('intact') form of knowledge. In the process, they activate a concept of tradition (which is able to produce unmediated, 'intact' knowledge), but at the expense of deactivating modernity (which is unable to do so). This binary returns us to a structure we have seen already which positions precolonial Aboriginal people as living out a bond between language and place, a bond that is interrupted or unsettled by modern conditions. In Davis and Prescott's research, in other words, the south of Australia is 'empty' because of the arbitrariness of the sign—because modernity produces mediation which interrupts the once stable or 'intact' relationship between signifier (language, knowledge) and signified (place, territory). This becomes a working assumption for them which determines not just which Aboriginal people they speak to, but what Aboriginal knowledges really matter.

Thus, in the context of AMIC's need to produce stability in a national framework full of 'risks', Davis and Prescott invoke a binary which relies on the assumption that stability is no longer with us (or at least, is diminishing). There is no longer a stable relationship between language, knowledge and place and, hence, no longer a 'full' or complete map of 'Aboriginal Australia' to be had. Their project was seen as contributing to the national desire for 'reconciliation',[42] in spite of the fact that they went on to produce a troubling irreconcilability between two kinds of Australia: the 'traditional' and the 'modern': the present and the absent ('lost forever'). Their mapping, in other words, provides an image of a divided nation, at least for Aboriginal people. Thus, even when 'dispassionate' academics attempt to settle things down in the name of reconciliation, they may at the same time unleash a certain level of unsettlement—quite literally, if one thinks of Davis's image of an 'empty', dispossessed (unable-to-be-possessed) southern Australia.

What we have with Davis and Prescott's work, then, is not a separation of Aboriginal people from property rights, but an attempt to restrict the influence of Aboriginal possession by designating 'traditional' occupation as the only legitimate way to land ownership. This return to the 'traditional' can very well be accompanied by a certain fascination with its features which naturalises or 'premodernises' Aboriginal people in a process which some commentators have designated as 'primitivism'. For anthropologist Andrew Lattas and historian Nicholas Thomas, for example, such 'primitivism' is simply a form of neocolonial racism, in that it locks Aboriginal people into a form of otherness which modernity needs, and which it therefore refuses to breach.[43] Our own view, however, is that 'primitivism' is not so much an end in itself as a symptom of a broader perception of Aboriginal practice in modern Australia. The entanglement of Aboriginal belief in sacredness and Aboriginal claims for property that we had noted earlier produces a certain kind of crisis for non-Aboriginal Australians. One may wish that claims for property could be dealt with 'rationally', but spiritual belief (and all the trappings that go with it: secrecy, unknowability, etc.) is always there to solicit that wish. Alternatively, in the struggle against this entanglement, one may become nostalgic for a moment when spiritual belief apparently stood by itself—since Aboriginal claims for property are seen nowadays to belong only in a modern, bureaucratic context. This modern context is held responsible for the corruption of the sacred (in its imagined 'original' or pure form), and it is this which results in the production of an image of 'Aboriginal bureaucracy' as 'monstrous'. What is called 'primitivism', then, is nothing more than an attempt to repudiate this context, to drive this 'monstrous' reality—this *modern* reality—away.

The struggle to disentangle Aboriginal beliefs from claims to property is played out whenever a mining company, for example, negotiates with an Aboriginal community over mining rights. A fascinating account of this is presented by Tony Grey, founder of Pancontinental Mining (Pancon), in his book *Jabiluka: The Battle to Mine Australia's Uranium* (1994). Recalling Durkheim some eighty years after the event, Grey expresses his concern about 'the relationship between the continent's original inhabitants and the modern world'.[44] Yet it is this relationship and, in particular, the bureaucratic formations it activates, which presents Grey with nothing but problems. Pancon, seeking to establish the right to mine uranium in the Northern Territory, is immediately confronted by the Aboriginal Land Rights Act, NT (1976)—an Act being put to use at that time by the Gagadju people for a land claim which covered the proposed mining site, Jabiluka. The power this Act gave to Aboriginal people to veto mining operations meant that Pancon soon found itself locked into protracted negotiations with the Northern Lands Council (NLC), who were acting on the Gagadju's behalf. Grey begins confidently enough, predicting a familiar enough gestation period: 'if we could get to the negotiating table with the NLC we felt able to conclude an agreement within nine months'.[45] Negotiations last much longer than this, however: long enough to make Grey consider them 'completely outside the usual framework of negotiation in the business world'.[46] Dealing with the NLC, in fact, generates such a level of uncertainty for Grey (in relation to Pancon's fortunes on the stock market) that it 'became a worry just to read the newspapers'.[47] What Grey experiences here is the power of 'Aboriginal bureaucracy' not so much to thwart but to determine the interests of a powerful, international company.[48] Under the sway of this kind of Aboriginal determination Grey experiences a massive loss of power, becoming, ultimately, unrecognisable to himself: 'I was the representative of a uranium producer which wasn't one. I felt like a phantom'.[49] The uncanny comes into play here with a vengeance where, at the moment of his confrontation with 'Aboriginal bureaucracy', the head of a mining company—far from experiencing the confirmation of that powerful identity—disappears into thin air.

For Grey, in an important sense the Northern Lands Council is not 'Aboriginal': it is apparently subjected to, even manipulated by, the views of anti-uranium activists and other non-Aboriginal lobby groups. The chairman of the NLC, Gularrwuy Yunipingu, comes to symbolise for Grey the tension of this relationship between a manipulating modernity and a subjected Aboriginality:

> I could see the anguish in his soul. A proud leader of his people in a modern world, he was just as trapped in the vice of white manipulation as any of his ancestors had ever been. He knew that all whites were disposed to use Aboriginal people as pawns in their own struggles. He had learned that the protestations of assistance from the so-called enlightened elements in white society were no less self-interested than the assertions by miners of the economic benefits from mining.[50]

It is because of this perceived level of 'manipulation' at work in 'Aboriginal bureaucracy' that Grey turns back to an image of traditional or original Aboriginality. Yunipingu is a 'natural leader' because 'local concerns were paramount'. He, and his family, embody naturalness: as they dance, the movements of his children seem to Grey 'so much more natural than I had ever seen in children before'.[51] Grey's enthrallment with the 'naturalness' of certain Aboriginal people leads him to return to the pre-Tindale, colonial view of Aboriginal people as naturally dispossessed, as nomadic—a view which relies on the disentangling of spiritual belief from property rights: 'within Aboriginal culture there is no ownership and possession of land as Europeans know it. An Aboriginal feels part of the land, in a sense consubstantial with it through a mystical, timeless connection originating in the Dreamtime. The land allows an Aboriginal to touch immortality'.[52]

So Grey's concern about the relationship between Aboriginal people and the modern world works itself out by seeing the latter as simply 'manipulating' the former, to generate bureaucratic structures which delay negotiations. These structures work to produce Aboriginal property rights which, at the very least, compromise the privileges that normally attend exploration and mining licences. This perception drives Grey into a mode of 'primitivism' in which dialogue can only be resumed because everyone now appears to be securely in their place (Aboriginal people are 'local', albeit dispossessed, while mining companies are global and in possession). Thus, 'primitivism' is a response to a broader anxiety associated with a (mis)recognition of the relationship between Aboriginal people and the modern world which sees Aboriginal empowerment as a form of corruption of an identity that was once 'pure'. And yet the non-Aboriginal enactment of a return to an 'original' Aboriginality by no means settles the issue. In this 'primitivist' fantasy, Aboriginal people may not have any property, but they still have belief, a level of spiritual belief that Grey is deeply attracted to, but which then reminds him of his own dispossession:

> Listening to this deeply spiritual man [Gularrwuy Yunipingu] caused me to reflect on the present dilemma of religion in white society. The supremacy of science over traditional religious explanations of phenomena, together with some spectacularly bad policy decisions, had secularised most of our society. The result is, for many, the closing off of formal or ritual outlets to express the spiritual dimension, often leading to frustrations or even bizarre perversions. This is not so with Aboriginal people. A paradox exists in that members of the white community often cannot tolerate spiritual expression when it comes from the institutional church but relate very strongly to it when it comes from indigenous people.[53]

The 'primitivist' perception yearns for an arrangement in which Aboriginal people have spiritual belief (sacredness) but no property rights—which would distinguish them from modern non-

Aboriginal people, who have property rights but no spiritual beliefs (secularity). But when this structure is disrupted—in particular, when modern Aboriginal people have spiritual beliefs *and* property rights (a marriage that 'Aboriginal bureaucracy' encourages)— then a certain form of resentment materialises. Aboriginal people become the same as non-Aboriginal people in that they, too, are identified through property (the rights of which are bureaucratically mediated). But they also have more than non-Aboriginal people in that this identification is premised upon spiritual beliefs, which secular non-Aboriginal people now lack. The entanglement of spiritual beliefs and property rights within a modern Aboriginal framework gives those property rights an intensity that secularised non-Aboriginal people simply cannot lay claim to. The resentment which materialises out of this structure lies in the recognition that Aboriginal people have too much in both spheres—too many property rights and too much spirituality—and this is especially so when the one functions to intensify the other. This mutual intensification, as we saw with Tony Grey, can be regarded as a way of making Aboriginal property peculiar to itself, especially if we remember that the word 'peculiar' (from the Latin *peculiaris*, of private property) was once used to describe the exemption enjoyed by the parish or church from the jurisdiction of its surroundings.

We have already noted the strange circumstances that come to enable non-Aboriginal people to identify themselves as lacking in relation to Aboriginal people, to see Aboriginal people as having more than they do. A more conventional view would focus on non-Aboriginal perceptions which, rightly, see Aboriginal people as having less: poorer housing, poorer health, fewer opportunities, less freedom. Far from producing resentment, this perception produces sympathy and 'guilt'. Yet the modern entanglement of sacredness and property rights in the field of 'Aboriginal politics' enables non-Aboriginal resentment to flourish at the same time, as if there is no apparent contradiction between these two positions. There is a perception that Aboriginal people can and will have access to more land surface than other Australians simply because of the peculiar amplification of the sacred—an amplification which is seen to happen all too easily under modern conditions. Thus, journalist Bill

Mandle can declare (not untypically) in a commentary in the *Canberra Times*:

> If Aborigines proclaim that a non-existent, never-having-existed, serpent might object to the turning of a sod; if a legend of irrationality beyond human comprehension, even if it be of human invention or, more likely, of divine provenance, by way of burning bush or a meaningful rock arrangement, can be summoned to prevent something, *then we pay attention*. Our secular, scientific, rational, relativist, non-prescriptive society goes to water.[54]

This resentment over the fact that Aboriginal people are now activated enough to command non-Aboriginal attention at will is another aspect of what we have called 'postcolonial racism'. It follows from a (mis)recognition that Aboriginal people now have too much: too much land surface (as in AMIC's estimations), too much unverifiable belief (as in Mandle's pronouncement), too much power over the nation's fortunes, too much of an ability to solicit the nation's attention, *too much charisma*. The paradox of postcolonial racism (which is why it is such an unstable form of racism) is that in the midst of resentment it can also be sympathetic towards, and even enthralled by, Aboriginal people in the ways just described. It can acknowledge that Aboriginal people do not have enough, while at the same time it can become anxious that they have (or may end up having) too much. In other words, postcolonial racism sees modern Aboriginal people as lacking (which produces sympathy and 'guilt') and as gaining (which produces anxiety and resentment) simultaneously: 'rudimentary', and 'gross'.

Where is the Sacred?

On the Reach of Coronation Hill

C ORONATION HILL—its Jawoyn (Djauan) Aboriginal name is 'Guratba'—is a not very imposing hill in remote northern Australia, in the southern reaches of the South Alligator River. This is *Crocodile Dundee* country. It lies in the midst of what has now become Stage III of Kakadu National Park, an area also registered as part of World Heritage, and subject to an Aboriginal land claim under existing land rights provisions, although Coronation Hill and its immediate surrounds have been excised and proclaimed a Conservation Zone. These designations have by no means prevented this part of the nation being mined—they were never restrictive or exclusive in this sense—and the Conservation Zone excision actually provided the pre-conditions for mining operations to proceed. In fact, in the case of Coronation Hill and its environs, mining ventures have operated more or less without restriction there since the early 1950s. This place is well used to the presence of mining companies. In 1985, however, the Northern Territory Aboriginal Sacred Sites Protection Authority registered the area around the Upper South Alligator River, including Coronation Hill, as a sacred site. At this time, mining interests in Coronation Hill had become large-scale, through the operations of Broken Hill Pty Company's (BHP's) Coronation Hill joint venture. This organisation had entered the area with the view to extracting massive amounts of gold, palladium and platinum. For the mining lobby and for some government interests Coronation Hill represented the richest single source of these minerals ever located in Australia. It was at the moment of Coronation Hill's registration as a sacred site, however, that the concerns of senior

Jawoyn custodians about these mining operations came to be expressed publically. In other words, the registration of Coronation Hill as a sacred site provided the means by which Aboriginal people could potentially exercise an exclusivity of use previously unattainable to them, which made this place notorious.

For the Jawoyn people Coronation Hill is part of an area which is associated with the Bula religious 'cult'. The term 'cult' was first offered, somewhat hesitantly, by Walter Arndt, a government Agricultural Research Officer based in the Northern Territory at Katherine. He was alerted to a local and striking form of spiritual belief when a near-fatal epidemic of hookworm-anaemia broke out in the Aboriginal labour camp he was supervising in 1955. An Aboriginal man in the camp explained to Arndt that the outbreak was due to disturbances from dynamite being used in uranium mining operations at a site some distance away, known to the Jawoyn as the 'Sickness Dreaming Place'. Arndt was warned that if mining operations did not stop, there would be cataclysmic results: everyone, including non-Aboriginal people, would die.[1]

Arndt responded to this somewhat disquieting news 'anthropologically', that is, he saw it as a fascinating form of local belief which needed to be recorded. Although an amateur anthropologist, Arndt was spurred into a frenzy of ethnographic activity, producing a detailed account of Bula, a male creation spirit which he described as 'a short thick-set man with short arms and legs'.[2] Arndt decided to bring his camera to a site located near to the mining operations to produce 'a complete colour slide coverage' which would then be shown to local Aboriginal people at 'free picture shows' where information might be gathered 'from the spontaneous remarks of the audience as the slides are shown'.[3] Arndt took more than eighty slides 'in a hectic 48 hours', presenting them to Aboriginal audiences 'at several places'; all these audiences recognised the 'Sickness Dreaming Place' and 'were satisfied that the mining operations had not damaged it'.[4] Aboriginal people were agreed that the site belonged to a particular family, and this helped Arndt find his first informants. What is arresting about this account is the way in which a modern technology, photography, was used as a means of bringing the 'truth' of a sacred site—that it had not been damaged by mining

—back to its Aboriginal custodians. In turn, the photographs enabled the truth of Aboriginal spiritual belief to be made apparent to Arndt, since, because he now had local Aboriginal informants to talk to face-to-face, he could rule out 'the possibility of a hoax'.[5]

Yet although the possibility of a 'hoax' is almost immediately discounted here, Arndt's elaboration of the Bula 'cult' installed some 'original' uncertainties which would return to haunt the later disputes over Coronation Hill. Firstly, as we have noted, the Bula sites that Arndt recorded are located at Sleisbeck and not Coronation Hill which lies some distance away. Arndt did, however, specify an extensive area associated with the 'Sickness Country'. Secondly, Arndt suggested that aspects of the cult 'must be of quite recent origin', no older than his informant: that is, 'not much more than 90 years old'.[6] Arndt emphasised the 'transitional' character of the Bula 'cult', seeing it as a spiritual belief which is still evolving in a post-contact environment. For Arndt, the 'modern-ness' of the Bula 'cult' by no means diminished its truth value. More to the point, it gave it a certain activated status where, like his informant's family, the 'cult' is 'still very much alive and is of future value and interest'.[7] So even in its first moment of recording, the question 'Where is the sacred?' remains unclear. Moreover, this question already operates in a modern context which, paradoxically, sees the Bula 'cult' as continuing to evolve even under modern conditions. In other words, the 'cult' has a traditional component, which works to keep it intact even after contact; and yet at the same time, aspects of it continue to change and adapt in a way which makes Arndt regard it as 'transitional' and evolving. These two apparently opposite features—that it is intact, and yet 'transitional'—can allow us to write the following equation in relation to this predicament: tradition is (not) modern.

By the early 1980s two sites which were known to be places where Bula entered the ground were registered by the Northern Territory's official site recording authority, the Aboriginal Sacred Sites Protection Authority. Soon afterwards, other discrete sites were placed on the official sacred sites register. By 1985 the registration of a number of discrete sites gave way to the classification of the 'Upper

South Alligator Bula Complex', which incorporated Coronation Hill. This sacred 'site' covered some 250 square kilometres. It was, in fact, a 'complex' of interconnected sites covered by Bula's 'sphere of influence'.[8] The registration marked a new way of recording sacredness, one which turned away from the restrictions implicit in a site or a 'spot', in response to an overhanging query about the limits of sacred effects.[9]

The registration also dealt with that part of the Bula 'cult' associated with Ngan-mol, an essence found in human bodily fluids but also a term used by the Jawoyn to refer to mineral deposits in the earth. So, for example, when gold was found at Coronation Hill by mining operatives, the Jawoyn understood this to be a trace of the body of Bula (or his wives). In this context, then, we might wonder: is this term 'Ngan-mol' traditional, or is it modern? At best, we could think of it as a 'transitional' term (following Arndt), as a term which both coheres and unsettles the connection between language and place. That connection is never just 'arbitrary' (to recall Muecke's arrangement), but it also never remains completely intact. According to anthropologists who had worked more recently with the Jawoyn, Ian Keen and Francesca Merlan, the discovery of gold at Coronation Hill confirmed an already-existing Jawoyn knowledge about Bula's 'sphere of influence'.[10] In this sense, then, mining implicated itself in the realisation of sacredness. Now the usual response from commentators with mining sympathies is that Aboriginal people, for purely opportunistic reasons, 'invented' this connection between Bula (Ngan-mol) and Coronation Hill (gold)—a response which would see this connection as an example of the modern arbitrariness of the sign. But our point would be that a modern technological practice, large-scale mining activity, functions here very much as photography had functioned for Arndt: far from rendering the connection between sacredness and place 'arbitrary', it gives it a certain truth. In other words, mining paradoxically functions as a way of verifying the sacred, which happens at the very moment that it places sacredness under threat. We can note a more general point about sacredness: that it is quite often realised as a topic or a claim only at the moment at which it is about to be desecrated, which may well explain why so many claims are made about sacredness in modern times. One can, accordingly, never hope to establish a 'complete' record of sacred sites; there is, in fact, no need to speak about sites which are not being (or which are not about to be) threatened. Indeed, it is quite possible that the number of actual sacred sites always exceeds the number on official registers.

We have already remarked on the approach taken by S. L. Davis and J. R. V. Prescott to territorial registration. In their chapter on 'Southwest Arnhem Land' they consider that the registration of Coronation Hill as part of a 'complex' of sites amounts to 'an incremental approach' intended to 'expand' Jawoyn property rights over the South Alligator Valley.[11] For them, the Jawoyn people are incremental or 'expansionist'. Davis and Prescott argue that the Jawoyn come to occupy land previously owned by the 'Wulwulam group who are now 'deceased', thus wilfully extending their 'territoriality over vacant territory'.[12] An allegory of colonisation is acted out here, with the Jawoyn in this account taking on the role usually ascribed to whites—settling in a place designated by Davis and Prescott as *terra nullius*, an empty place. The striking feature of this account is that what is otherwise perfectly familiar to Davis and Prescott—the fact that modern, non-Aboriginal interests are always expansive and incremental—is transformed into a structure to be disapproved of when it is applied to Aboriginal people. What makes them anxious is their perception that the Jawoyn are not only expanding their territory, but expanding the scope and range of their spiritual beliefs in an unruly, 'improper' or illegitimate way. Once again, 'Aboriginal bureaucracies' (the Aboriginal Land Rights Act, NT [1976], as well as National Park designations) are to blame here for having 'acted as a catalyst to activate succession by the Jawoyn'.[13] But the real problem for Davis and Prescott turns back to Arndt's point about the 'recentness' of aspects of the Bula 'cult'. For them, Jawoyn succession to land incorporating Coronation Hill is illegitimate not only because 'traditions are being manufactured quite quickly', but also because the 'recentness' of those traditions means that somehow they are not traditional *enough*:

> It [bureaucratic activity] may also have prematurely brought it [succession] into a stage whereby the attendant details of sites, songs and ceremonies have not been sufficiently developed or restructured as to

adequately support the Jawoyn claims to possessing active traditions for the area or to sustain their efforts to exercise territoriality in respect of the area.[14]

For Arndt, what had been a 'transitional' form of spiritual belief is here characterised as 'premature': the tone of the intervention has changed over the space of thirty years. It is tempting to regard Arndt's investigations into the Bula 'cult' in the 1950s as a moment of anthropological innocence, a mere exercise in curiosity since there was nothing to be gained or lost by this amateur anthropologist in claiming that Jawoyn traditions were perpetually in formation. But Davis and Prescott's book redeploys this innocent designation in a context where nothing now is not political. Let us return to the quote for a moment. The slippage from 'transitional' (1962) to 'premature' (1992) amounts to a substitution of a model of change for its own sake with a model of development: for Davis and Prescott, the Jawoyn's traditions are not developed enough to produce the kind of coherent connection between language and place that their notion of legitimate succession to land depends upon. Yet Davis and Prescott do not seem to disallow the possibility that this connection may one day become coherent, the pressures of modernity notwithstanding. The strange thing about their account of Coronation Hill, then, is that they conclude it by consigning 'tradition' to the future.

Francesca Merlan has noted that commentaries on Aboriginal claims about Coronation Hill are usually framed within a binary of 'tradition' and 'modern-ness', a binary which tends to separate the two from each other as if each component is entirely distinct and autonomous.[15] Aboriginal 'modern-ness' is thus understood here as involving either a loss of traditions or an 'invention' of traditions, or both. For Merlan, however, traditional belief and modern contexts fold into each other in dynamic ways. As she says of her work (commissioned by the Resource Assessment Commission) with anthropologist Ian Keen and the Jawoyn, 'most of what is known about the "Bula" tradition has been learned precisely in relation to intrusions, mainly mining and pastoral development, in the context of [the] specific historical relations of white-black interaction'.[16] This observation, however, does not entirely unsettle the binary that troubles Merlan, for she has her own professional investment in a notion of 'tradition' even as she recognises its subjection to change. The dispute over Coronation Hill involved a central problem of representation: who were the legitimate claimants? This is a way of asking, in effect, 'who were the Jawoyn?' Senior custodians were opposed to mining because of their spiritual belief in Bula; but some younger Jawoyn (who later gained a more public profile through the Jawoyn Association) were more inclined to negotiate and work with mining interests—producing a generational difference which, in the spirit of the differend, was often seen as irreconcilable. So how does a sympathetic anthropologist negotiate this difference? An alignment of one sort or another has to be realised, and in the very act of alignment the binary of 'tradition' and 'modern-ness' is reconstituted. Merlan's alignment is with the senior custodians and with their spiritual beliefs, which are allowed to remain intact no matter how malleable they may be (or may have become) under modern conditions. Actually, the differend does not quite apply here, because by reconstituting the binary she had been critiquing Merlan goes on to imply that younger, pro-mining Jawoyn have disenfranchised themselves from a local, place-based identity. That is, she necessarily produces a structure where one side is legitimate (the older, senior custodians) and one side is not. Thus, she questions the 'extent to which those who have worked for the mining company . . . *do* have a vision of community, or a distinct vision of community . . . it seems to me that questions of community do not figure very explicitly in the workers' discussions about advantages they think mining would offer them . . .'[17] In other words, Merlan's alignment with Bula produces, almost in spite of itself, a constituency of Jawoyn (a younger, more 'modern', pro-mining generation) who are (not) Jawoyn because they appear to eschew the cohering structure of 'community'—a structure made coherent through its bond to a sacred site.

The fascinating thing about the Coronation Hill case is that it demonstrated the sheer impossibility of occupying a non-aligned or non-partisan position in relation to it. At the same time, it produced a whole range of objections against people who *were* partisan, such as those anthropologists who seemed sympathetically to go along

with the Jawoyn belief that Bula is a creation spirit who, if disturbed, could 'shake 'im this country' (to give the title of a 1986
video produced by the Aboriginal Sacred Sites Protection Authority
on behalf of the Jawoyn). Merlan's account, for example, notes that
the Jawoyn had reorganised their understanding of Bula's effects in
the context of modern conditions, which leads her to quote Aboriginal commentators who had said that if Bula is disturbed, then
'earthquake, fire and flood will affect "Sydney, Melbourne, overseas", the known limits of the world'.[18] The point is that although
Merlan provides a modern articulation of Jawoyn spiritual belief,
with all of its potential reach, she nevertheless leaves the belief itself
intact: the legitimacy of the belief in Bula himself is (in line with the
differend) not at issue. For some other commentators, however, it
certainly was an issue, one which mobilised an intense scepticism of
almost every claim made about Coronation Hill except their own.
The most publicised of these commentators was the anthropologist
Ron Brunton, who at the time was head of the Environmental
Policy Unity of the right-wing think-tank, the Institute of Public
Affairs.

Brunton goes along with Merlan's general point, that Aboriginal traditions 'are dynamic and innovatory'.[19] In fact, he argues
against the view that Aboriginal people are bound by traditional
beliefs which never change. This view, he suggests, amounts to the
promotion of 'an ideology designed to protect the legitimacy of
authority by blocking challenges based on religious innovation to
the position of the senior men'.[20] We can note that the origins of this
protective 'ideology' are never made entirely clear: is it activated
internally by Aboriginal 'senior men' to maintain their authority? Is
it imposed externally by 'Aboriginal bureaucracies' such as the
Northern Lands Council which, by opposing mining at Coronation
Hill, happened to underwrite the authority of those 'senior men'?
Or—given Prime Minister Bob Hawke's decision to rule out mining
at Coronation Hill—is it more broadly based than this? Let us make
the point that Brunton's task is to push any such 'ideology' aside in
order to make the connection between 'authority' and traditional
belief illegitimate. In other words, he wants to enlighten Aboriginal
people and non-Aboriginal people alike to a structure—one he

identifies as 'modern' and progressive—through which Aboriginal authority (that was 'protected' under the framework of tradition) can now only be received sceptically. The belief held by senior Jawoyn men that to disturb Bula would cause an apocalyptic level of destruction is, for Brunton, precisely an example of how traditional modes of authority can work ideologically to 'protect' those people's interests. To be modern, he implies, is to be sceptical of this arrangement:

> A number of Jawoyn want the mine to go ahead. They are sceptical about any retaliation from Bula, pointing out that nothing happened after the earlier mining at Coronation Hill.
>
> This scepticism is a positive development, part of the process whereby Aborigines make a creative accommodation to the opportunities our culture can provide to them . . .[21]

In this account, sceptical Aboriginal people can 'accommodate' themselves to modern Australia. That is, through the development of scepticism they can become like 'us'. Part of the problem with Brunton's argument is that the level of scepticism he wants to mobilise in effect does away with cultural difference. It is, essentially, assimilationist. It is a way of making us all the same: now, none of us, Aboriginal people and non-Aboriginal people alike, can lay claim to tradition and the kinds of authority that went along with it.

How can Aboriginal traditions—spiritual belief, for example—be mobilised in a modern, sceptical Australia? For Brunton, the kind of traditions mobilised at Coronation Hill are all the more scandalous because they seem to be so recent. Worse, the apparent recent incarnations of Aboriginal belief, in this case the belief in Bula's location at Coronation Hill, seem to have activated it beyond all 'legitimate' proportions. Thus he comments:

> in less than thirty years, 'Sickness Country' has grown to nearly eight times its former size and been surrounded with a swag of new restrictions. In the 1950s and 1960s there was no concern about mining in the Sickness Country as such. And the anthropological consultants . . . say that now there is even a suggestion that Bulas 'are "breeding" under the ground'.[22]

This apparently excessive amplification of sacredness is, for Brunton, tied up with his claim that the Jawoyn belief in Bula is little more than a decade old. Now for Walter Arndt, the Jawoyn belief in Bula's location at Sleisbeck was 'of quite recent origin', possibly about ninety years old. But for Brunton, the Jawoyn belief in Bula's location at Coronation Hill is even more recent. This is indeed a cause for scepticism, but only in the context of having once believed:

> there can be little doubt that the vast majority of Australians believe that traditional Aboriginal religious beliefs and practices are of great antiquity, and that this belief has provided much of the legitimacy for legislation protecting sites. In *Aborigines and Environmental Myths* I noted that this belief was even held by highly educated Australians with a strong interest in Aboriginal culture. Australians' willingness to protect sites associated with beliefs only 10 years old is likely to be considerably less than their willingness to protect sites 10,000 years old—particularly if such protection could harm one of the nation's most important industries.

This is a fascinating statement, one which buys into a common view of what might constitute a 'tradition', and we can spend a moment wondering about it. If tradition is 'traditional' then it is believable: what Brunton had identified as an 'ideology designed to protect authority' earlier on, is here identified (albeit sceptically through Brunton's tone) as a truth which non-Aboriginal people as well as Aboriginal people may well have subscribed to (although in this case one may still not believe in what might happen if Bula is disturbed). But if tradition is not 'traditional', then truth reverts back to a 'designed' ideology and needs to be treated sceptically. We can note two features of this argument. Firstly, there is this implication that people—Aboriginal people and non-Aboriginal people (who are not distinguished in Brunton's argument)—believe too readily. Why is it that a sceptical and rational modernity allows something apparently irrational, Aboriginal spiritual belief, so much space, so much presence? Why does Aboriginal spiritual belief command so much attention from modern Australia? We can simply observe here that Brunton appears baffled by this apparent contradiction. Our second point, however, is that there is something quite arbitrary underwriting his distinction between belief (traditional) and scepticism (modernity). For Walter Arndt, to come across a 'transitional' tradition, aspects of which are only ninety years old, was a little unsettling but the possibility of a 'hoax' was ruled out. For Brunton, a tradition which is ten years old is simply insufficiently developed to be believed—immature rather than 'premature'—whereas a tradition of 10 000 years receives everyone's blessing. So who arbitrates over the kind of time-frame which makes a tradition believable and proper? We can suggest that this is another place where the arbitrariness of the sign makes its presence felt, where the relation tradition bears to what is sometimes called 'time depth' can never entirely be settled, even when one is sure that such a relation ought 'properly' to exist.

The point is that belief (tradition) and scepticism (modernity) are by no means able to be disentangled from each other in this way. To operate as if they could be disentangled, as Brunton does, is to produce a mystifying structure. Not only does a sceptical modernity inexplicably entertain the kind of 'ideology' designed to 'protect' traditional forms of spiritual belief; it also enables the 'least' traditional of beliefs, as in the case of Bula, to become the most 'protected' of all! Having broken down legitimate but traditional connections between authority and belief, a sceptical modernity can only respond by claiming any attempt to retrieve or reorganise these connections to be 'illegitimate'. This arrangement does not work to set belief aside by any means. In fact, it can participate in the proliferation of categories of 'belief' that are then each taken as cause for anxiety (which is exactly how 'cults' are so often experienced these days). But we need not polarise scepticism and belief quite so dramatically. Indeed, the postcoloniality of Australia produces a much more agnostic relationship to this structure: believing (in tradition, in Bula, in belief itself) and not believing at the same time. One can feel the effects of belief even as one remains sceptical, for instance—and certainly, Bula produced a range of often traumatic effects with which even the most sceptical of non-Aboriginal Australians were forced to deal. To be sceptical and modern, in other words, is by no means to be protected from the effects of belief and the traditions (however recent they may be) that they mobilise.

We can see this if we turn again to Brunton, whose commentaries on Coronation Hill actually realised the kind of disturbances of which Bula would have been proud. In an article titled 'Controversy in the Sickness Country: the battle over Coronation Hill' (1991), Brunton describes the fall-out over claims he had made about the sacred site dispute. His faith in truth and objectivity (that is, scepticism) leads Brunton to see himself, and a few others, as 'a minority' in the profession of anthropology.[23] Brunton, much like other conservative commentators in postcolonial Australia, then appropriates the discourses of a 'minority politics' for himself. For example, he appeals for truth-value to an unnamed 'senior and expert anthropologist' from Harvard and to the 'respected and influential' critic, P. P. McGuinness.[24] The strange irony is that Brunton thus informs his 'minority' status by turning to the kind of 'ideology designed to protect the legitimacy of authority' he had earlier critiqued in relation to Aboriginal people: he appeals, in other words, to the inviolability of senior men. Brunton goes on to describe a visit to the Anthropology Department in the School of General Studies at the Australian National University. In the tearoom, he becomes 'the focus of indignation' from others; when he talks about 'an obligation to tell the truth', people snigger as if 'I had broken a taboo'.[25] After this, a seminar is arranged with Brunton as a guest speaker, alongside Ian Keen, amongst others. After Brunton finishes his paper, Keen fires 'the first shot'; later on, he hears from a 'witness' that people had called him a number of derogatory names. On the other hand, a few people 'expressed varying degrees of sympathy with statements I had made'.[26] The rest of Brunton's article elaborates his embattled position: the 'battle over Coronation Hill' is his own, in fact, and it is outlined in lurid detail in this account. The uncanny thing about this article, then, is that this particular commentator comes to occupy the kind of positioning we might associate with 'being Aboriginal': he utilises the discourse of 'minority politics', appealing to the authority of 'senior men'; he is received 'sceptically' by those around him (his own scepticism notwithstanding); he is derided and insulted; but there are at least a few sympathetic supporters. Even his testimonial about Coronation Hill is subjected to the transgressions of anthropological curiosity from 'outside'. A post-graduate student tapes the seminar, with Brunton's permission, but after consulting with another anthropologist she refuses to make the tape available to him. So the seminar room becomes a site of significance, which estranges Brunton even as it includes him: it produces a certain kind of dispossession on his behalf. In the light of all this, we might ask: where exactly is the 'Sickness Country' of his article's title? And how far does Bula reach? The creation spirit's 'sphere of influence' may, in this account, have spread at least as far as a seminar room at the Australian National University which, when Brunton visits it, is traumatically unsettled. Remembering the point we have made already, that the postcolonial sacred site is known primarily through its effects, it is thus not beyond the realms of imagination to suggest that there is a closer connection between Brunton and Bula than the former would admit to. Indeed, what we have here is the advocate of a modern form of scepticism becoming nothing less than an actual vehicle for, or an uncanny manifestation of, the disruptive force of 'a short thick-set man with short arms and legs' he professes not to believe in.

Let us be in no doubt that Bula—in spite of (or even, because of) the scepticism of modern Australians—has had real effects, activating the site of Coronation Hill and spreading its 'sphere of influence' across the broadest possible base. In 1988 Kenneth Maddock made the following prediction:

> I believe that the Coronation Hill dispute could expand to become even bigger than the Noonkanbah dispute some years ago in Western Australia . . . The Noonkanbah dispute petered out once it became clear that mining prospects were poor . . . [whereas] the deep and peculiar significance of Bula introduces an explosive and unpredictable element. Without Bula, Coronation Hill may never have hit the headlines.[27]

Here, it is Bula, not mineral wealth, which makes Coronation Hill 'peculiar', and the 'peculiarity' of Bula is seen to be much more decisive in the spread of this site's influence. The point is that Bula did not just 'hit the headlines', which he certainly did; he also determined the perceptions of Australian business and governmentality. Western Mining's Hugh Morgan produced the kind of cataclysmic response that we have already seen, as if Bula could literally activate a whole range of other prospective mining sites across the country:

> Already we see Premier Carmen Lawrence of WA, herself a former Aboriginal Affairs Minister, seeking to ward off the spirit of Bula II, by threatening special legislation with respect to Hammersley's Marandoo iron ore project. At Yakabindi, Dominion Mining Ltd is suddenly threatened with Bula III, and similarly the Premier has committed her Government to amending legislation if necessary.[28]

Morgan imagines a nation populated with Bulas, bearing out those anthropologists, noted earlier, who had observed that this creation spirit is somehow able to 'breed'. His view is not entirely untypical of conservative responses at the time: the then Liberal Opposition spokesman on Aboriginal Affairs, Dr Michael Wooldridge, had also said: 'If the Government thinks this is a one-off—that there'll be no further Bula sites—then it is quite wrong, because . . . any area of significance, no matter how trivial to Aboriginal people, can be declared a sacred site'.[29] A headline in the *Weekend Australian* captured this kind of cataclysmic amplification of sacredness by similarly noting, ' "Sickness Country" may become a national epidemic'.[30]

Even opposition to Bula in the name of modern business can find itself drawing on 'primitivist' rhetoric, as if the one cannot now conceive of itself without the other. For example, the then Labor Treasurer John Kerin expressed his support for mining at Coronation Hill in this way: 'It is very clear to me that this issue goes beyond Coronation Hill *per se*. In the eyes of Australia's businessmen, particularly the mining community but infiltrated throughout the business community generally, I see this very much as a totem issue for Australian business'.[31] We can note how the phrase 'totem issue' slips into this account of modern Australian business, the implication being that if mining goes ahead at Coronation Hill then business will prosper through a kind of renewed unification. That is, it will cohere as a 'kinship group' under the influence of what Durkheim calls the 'protecting genius' of the totem.[32] In fact, the totem works to provide not only kinship but also territoriality: it is invoked as an image which will magically keep business interests in place (including in the place of Coronation Hill). It is, in other words, a precise example of Brunton's 'ideology', designed to protect the interests of senior men in the 'tribal' world of big business. Interestingly enough, when Prime Minister Bob Hawke eventually vetoed mining activity at Coronation Hill in June 1991, to protect Jawoyn beliefs, the Melbourne *Age* ran an editorial which then located the notion of the totem at the heart of the Government itself:

> Coronation Hill, regrettably, has been imbued with a symbolic significance far in excess of its intrinsic value as a gold and platinum mine to be exploited, as a natural wilderness to be conserved and, some would say, as an Aboriginal site to be protected forever. It has also become a political totem for the embattled Prime Minister, Mr Hawke, whose emotional commitment to exclude mining in deference to Aboriginal beliefs and wishes has finally prevailed over a divided Cabinet. It was a victory for the spirit of Bula and the will of Bob Hawke over economic imperatives and political compromise.[33]

Bob Hawke had forcefully overruled a majority Cabinet vote in order to veto mining at Coronation Hill. And yet the decision was seen as 'soft' and emotional rather than 'hard' and pragmatic, not unexpected from an increasingly feminised Prime Minister ('old jellyback'). There was even a suggestion that Hawke was in favour of Bula to ease strained relations with his son Steve, whose co-authored book *Noonkanbah* (1989) had advocated the protection of sacred sites from mining interests.[34] Hawke becomes a 'sentimental' Prime Minister, known to have wept in public over issues of racism, who allows a 'hard' decision to be influenced by relations with his son, and who returns sacred sites to Aboriginal people— and yet he becomes forceful enough, charismatic enough ('the will of Bob Hawke'), to carry a minority vote. The *Age* editorial put this empowerment into a particular and most appropriate context. As well as recognising the already fantastic amplification of Coronation

Hill, this editorial again invoked the totem, raising the stakes of this amplification even further by constructing a 'kinship group' between Bula and the Prime Minister himself. By protecting Bula, this 'embattled' and emotional, feminised Prime Minister is, in turn, bestowed with enough power by Bula himself to cohere a divided Cabinet. This is the source of his charisma: a sacred site many hundreds of kilometres away. We can also note that Hawke's 'totem', which aligned him with Bula, worked directly against John Kerin's image of the 'kinship group' interests of business: a totem gained is a totem lost. So a spirit residing at a not very imposing hill in remote northern Australia eventually finds himself at the centre of the modern nation: his 'sphere of influence' is not just utterly unbounded, it is (if only for a moment, at least) utterly determining.

The Return of the Sacred

On Repatriation and Charisma

THE REPATRIATION by archaeologists and museums of sacred objects to Aboriginal people is another striking example of the 'return' of the Aboriginal sacred in contemporary Australia. Under the colonial logic of the late nineteenth century and early twentieth century, museums across metropolitan Australia had systematically collected and stored Aboriginal sacred objects. The collection of Aboriginal artefacts was undertaken on the assumption that Aboriginal people were a 'dying race', in which case the museum became the final resting place for objects now designated as 'relics'. This would seem to have been the last word on the matter, as if the status and location of these collected objects were finally 'settled': no longer part of an 'Aboriginal system' because they are now a part of the 'museum system'. But since the early 1970s the boundaries of ownership and authority that this arrangement assumes have been profoundly unsettled. The 'museum system' has by no means had the last word on the matter; the 'Aboriginal system' has talked back, soliciting museums by making claims, postcolonial claims, on their collections to which museums sooner or later are obliged to respond. This chapter will look at a number of accounts of the return of sacred objects to Aboriginal people: to see what is at stake, what is lost and what is gained, what restraints are mobilised when a 'return' is made, and what powers are unleashed.

In his important book *Hunters and Collectors: The Antiquarian Imagination in Australia* (1996), Tom Griffiths traces a genealogy of collecting Aboriginal artefacts and objects in colonial Victoria. The Epilogue to his book works to involve Griffiths himself, once a researcher at the Museum of Victoria, in the postcoloniality of object collection and its consequences. Griffiths gives an account of how he receives some 'secret/sacred' Aboriginal objects from the daughter of a colonial collector—belated objects which, although removed from the 'Aboriginal system' some time ago, were yet to be lodged in the 'museum system'. The role Griffiths is given here is essentially colonial after the event of colonialism, in that he is the one who delivers these objects to the museum. In the earlier frame of colonialism itself, the predicament Griffiths finds himself in would be relatively unproblematic: museums wanted these objects and collectors were happy to collect them. But after colonialism, his predicament is instead a source of anxiety, producing 'worries' instead of 'smiles'. Let us quote the relevant passage, beginning with Griffiths' receipt of these objects and the beginning of his journey with them to the museum:

> Even parcelled in a dusty box they were, I suspected, still full of power . . . During the long drive back to Melbourne I felt increasingly conscious of the boxes in the back of the station-wagon enclosing the secret/sacred objects. Whose were they? What meanings did they hold? What processes had brought them here, a process that now implicated me? I thought of a scene at the end of *Raiders of the Lost Ark*, a film about the archaeologist-adventurer Indiana Jones, where the immensely powerful ark of the covenant is casually wheeled into the vaults of a state museum. Was I participating in the dispossession of a people and the disenchantment of the world? It was while driving the sacred stones across Victoria that I first thought of doing this research.[1]

This wonderfully dramatic passage is full of ripe contradictions which speak to the unruly effects of the Aboriginal sacred in the postcolonial moment. Griffiths' sense of being 'implicated' in colonial processes is not debilitating but inspirational, enabling the very book he has just written: guilt, in other words, is quite literally productive. But what is most striking about this account is the way it 'talks up' this strange predicament. Griffiths immediately inscribes these belated objects with power: so much power, in fact, that their delivery to the museum may (in a phrase lifted from Durkheim's contemporary Max Weber) lead to 'the disenchantment of the world'. What does disenchantment refer to here, exactly? Is it related to Griffiths' sense of being 'implicated' in colonial processes (taking sacred objects to the museum) in a supposedly postcolonial moment? A certain kind of loss is articulated in this remark: by receiving sacred objects in this way at this time, the museum has lost something. Postcolonial museums, and their curators, repatriate: they return objects; they no longer collect in this way, and to be reminded that they might still be called upon to do this could indeed be 'disenchanting'. So at this point, his 'implication' in the colonial process of collecting objects is conceived abjectly rather than inspirationally. Yet Griffiths is none the less enchanted enough with these belated objects to inscribe them with immense power, apparently through nothing more than the authority of his own 'suspicions'. Later in the passage, these objects are directly compared to the 'immensely powerful' Ark of the Covenant in the Steven Spielberg film *Raiders of the Lost Ark* (1981), with Griffiths imagining himself returning sacred objects to a museum through a heroic popular narrative. Proximity to these objects thus produces both enchantment and disenchantment, inspiration and abjection. But whichever way it goes, the outcome is a dramatic articulation of charismatic power—charisma gained through those dusty objects, not because of their location in the 'Aboriginal system' (their 'authentic' location) but because of their position in the back of Griffiths' station-wagon. The German critic Walter Benjamin, in his essay on collecting, has this to say about the relationship between the collector and his collected objects: it is 'not that they come alive in him; it is he who lives in them'.[2] But in the postcolonial story that Griffiths tells it is difficult to decide which is which, which party animates and which party is animated.

Griffiths' book deals imaginatively with the concept of 'possession', taking it in precisely this double sense: that one can own an object and yet one can be owned by it at the same time. In order to produce the former position and keep one's authority over the collected object intact, that object has to be de-animated: rendered, to recall Raymond Williams' term, 'archaic'. Thus, Griffiths says, colonial collectors 'disdained the native informant and preferred to work with *mute "relics"* '.[3] Such relics become 'mute' because the 'native informant' is so completely removed from the object under possession: no input is allowed from the 'Aboriginal system'. But how 'mute' can a relic be? Elsewhere in his book Griffiths notes that 'dumb relics' were already 'raising deeply disturbing questions' for antiquarians and archaeologists, even in colonial times.[4] So even when it is removed from an 'Aboriginal system', a relic is never completely 'archaic': it always carries a residual force; it can never be fully de-animated. When the 'Aboriginal system' returns to the relic, of course—claiming sacred objects back from collectors, from museums—then obviously the relic is more than just residual. It has instead an emergent and even, in the view of some commentators, a dominant function. Under these postcolonial conditions, collectors can find themselves preoccupied with losing power because another kind of possession has come into play—the assumption that one can own an object (the assumption that ownership is settled) is solicited. Can the object be so activated by the 'Aboriginal system' that the collector not only feels owned by it but is obliged to respond to that form of possession in one way or another? Is this always going to produce a loss (of the collector's power)? We have already seen Griffiths become charismatic under the influence of sacred objects being taken from a colonial collection to a postcolonial museum. They produce abjection on the one hand and inspiration on the other: losses, certainly, but gains as well.

The discipline which has most often registered this range of responses to the repatriation of sacred objects is archaeology. Skeletal remains, of course, are not necessarily always sacred; burial archaeologist Colin Pardoe gives them a particular qualification when he notes, 'bones occupy a particular place in the physical world that is uneasily on the edge of the supernatural, the sacred, the taboo'.[5] Nevertheless, these objects are significant enough to be claimed back from archaeological collections by particular Aboriginal communities, thereby producing some of the most acrimonious debates over who is entitled to possess cultural property. At the beginning of the 1990s two emblematic episodes of skeletal repatriation opened up a set of available positions which archaeologists felt bound to occupy: the Museum of Victoria's repatriation of its Kow Swamp collection of human remains in 1990, and the so-called 'Mungo Lady' return of early 1992. The Mungo Lady's return was honoured with a ceremony which drew together the scattered descendants of her people: the Paakantji, the Mathi Mathi and the Ngiyampaa. Others were involved as well in this emotional return: 'There were tears, too, from some of the white people. Mr Alec Barnes, whose life was irrevocably changed by the discovery of Mungo woman's bones on his property, did not trust himself to speak'[6]—this man is animated enough by these relics to become mute! Also there, of course, were the archaeologists. The return was exemplary in the sense that participation was mutual and willing across parties that might previously have stood opposed to each other or even 'disdained' each other. The conciliatory nature of the return was represented through the arrangements for storing and accessing the remains. Mungo Lady was returned to a 'closed place', a locked safe in the Mungo National Park exhibition centre which could only be opened with two keys, one held by archaeologists, the other by local Aboriginal people. In this sense, she is hidden-for-all-to-see. A certain resolution to the tension between the secrecy usually ascribed to sacredness and the modern urge to disclose or make public is thus achieved through this closed-yet-open burial. A Melbourne *Age* editorial left little doubt about the exemplary significance of the event: 'The decision ... to give Mungo woman back is a sign that reconciliation, and negotiation, between Aboriginal beliefs and science may be possible'.[7]

The repatriation of Mungo Lady was a 'proper' return, read as a 'sign' or symptom of the broader project of reconciliation in Australia. But it came in the wake of the repatriation of the Kow Swamp collection, which spoke more to the impossibility of reconciliation between competing systems of possession. In August 1990 the Museum of Victoria repatriated Pleistocene human remains and other objects to the Echuca Aboriginal Co-operative. For eminent pre-historian John Mulvaney, this produced more 'worries' than 'smiles'; notably, it blocked the business of archaeology and 'compromised' the museum. The return was improper rather than proper, not least because archaeology's image of itself seemed to be shown no respect by the claimants. The 'intellectual freedom' of the archaeologist was unduly restricted by the Echuca claims; the 'international standing' of the museum and archaeology's imagined 'global significance' were substantially reduced by the unexpected rise to power of a local community; and to add insult to injury, archaeologists no longer seemed to know the whereabouts of what had so recently been under their full possession: 'Their subsequent fate remains obscure to all but the Echuca people'.[8] For Mulvaney, openness and closure cannot be hyphenated as they were with Mungo Lady: the 'obscure' consequences of the return of these remains to the local 'negates the spirit of open inquiry for all people'.[9] Note how archaeology talks up its self-image in this remark: imagining that its *own* 'obscure' projects, in fact, speak for 'all of us'. At the same time, Mulvaney's account is soaked in abjection, in the sense that at the very moment at which archaeology can find the sheer bravado to suggest that it speaks openly 'for all people' it experiences its own muteness. Mulvaney's pleas to deal with the Kow Swamp skeletal remains in his own way meet what he describes as a 'wall of silence': no one is listening.[10]

Mulvaney was not opposed to the repatriation of museum objects to Aboriginal people: he had long been an advocate for Aboriginal 'keeping places' in which these objects can be safely— that is, 'properly'—stored. This is where 'reconciliation' can happen but only because these objects, repatriated as they might be, at least in part *continue to remain under the logic of the 'museum system'*. This is a system which, having been able to accommodate 'keeping places' under postcolonial conditions, ensures that those objects (like Mungo Lady) are closed-yet-open. Mulvaney's problem with Kow Swamp is that these remains slip out of that system and become 'obscure': there is no openness left for the museum and archaeologists to claim back. From Mulvaney's point of view, the Kow Swamp repatriation was improper in the sense that it produced nothing other than loss: closure. Colonial collectors had 'disdained the native informant' in order to render their objects 'mute', but here it is Mulvaney's discipline of archaeology that experiences such disdain when contemporary Aboriginal people return to the scene. The skeletal remains become 'mute relics' once more in an uncanny mirroring of the colonial situation that Griffiths had described.

We can see how Mulvaney's abjection is revisited in a more recent response to repatriation by the Professor of Archaeology at La Trobe University, Tim Murray. Murray has been concerned about 'the *forced* repatriation of cultural properties' in 1995 from La Trobe University to Aboriginal people in Tasmania, under action from the Tasmanian Aboriginal Land Council.[11] Clearly, this archaeologist is speaking from a position of reluctance: reluctance to lose possession. But how does he articulate this loss? Mulvaney had given archaeology the power to speak for 'all of us'; Tim Murray focuses this power by appealing to archaeology's capacity to speak for 'all Australians', that is, for the interests of the nation.[12] Let us note again just how imaginary this appeal actually is. Archaeology claims this power for itself—this incredible reach across Australia, this incredible ability to reach 'all of us'—in order then to be able to perform the loss of power brought upon it through Aboriginal claims for the return of their objects. Consistent with this point is archaeology's (equally imaginary) investment in its openness and pluralism, an investment which then enables it to categorise Aboriginal possession of objects as a form of closure. Those elements may even be destined for 'obscurity' once more, through yet another 'improper' burial: Murray is 'dismayed to learn that the elements of a repatriated collection had already been deposited in the waters of Lake Burberry'.[13] Since archaeology is connected synedochally (and wishfully) to the nation, as if they both share the same interests and ideals, everyone thus suffers as a result: 'the potential loss to all of us', Murray says, 'is surely great enough for us to do what we can to make sure that it does not happen again'.[14] In his discussions with the Tasmanian government, Murray talks up the openness of archaeology again and again, seeing it as emblematic of democracy at its most multicultural: 'we were promoting the expression of a wide range of cultural interests in the Aboriginal history of Australia, not just those of Aboriginal people or "scientists" . . . the best outcome should be respect for diverse ways in which we all make meanings about the human history of Australia'.[15] A discipline that may itself appear utterly 'obscure' to many Australians thus represents itself as emblematic of a democratic, pluralist nation state. Under these imaginings, Aboriginal people are coded as *un*Australian, standing for closure, standing against 'freedom' and 'diversity'. This is an increasingly familiar form of postcolonial racism, of course, in its view that these unAustralian Aboriginal people have now, since their claims on the La Trobe University material were honoured, gained more power than archaeology. For Murray, 'the gain of empowering Aborigines was seen to outweigh the loss of knowledge'.[16] Notice how 'knowledge' is kept suitably open here, rather than as something specific to the obscurities of archaeology. It is as if postcolonial conditions have produced a strange miscalculation, whereby Aboriginal people have gained at the expense of archaeology, which Murray can now characterise as 'marginalised'.[17] How uncannily fascinating it is when archaeology can be emblematic of the democratic nation and abjectly marginal at the same time!

Murray's commentary on the Tasmanian repatriation is intended to illustrate 'the potential for things to go badly wrong', at least for archaeology.[18] When one party's gain is read as the second party's loss, there is no possibility of reconciliation. And when that second party characterises itself as 'pluralist', open and able to speak for 'all of us', whereas Aboriginal people are seen as having only '*one* strategy for establishing the meanings of places or things', the outcome is seen as cataclysmic.[19] But do archaeologists and museum officials always respond so negatively to repatriation? Can repatriation ever be read as a gain for these seemingly embattled, 'marginalised' people? In his article 'Arches of Radii, corridors of power: reflections on current archaeological practice', Colin Pardoe offers a different point of view on the repatriation and reburial of human remains. He makes the point that 'proper', consultative archaeological practices do not produce the kinds of losses that Mulvaney and Murray mourn. In fact, Pardoe believes in quite the reverse, that they would produce gains without limits: 'If we exhibit good manners, is there anything in the pursuit of archaeology that we *cannot* do?'[20]

Christopher Anderson, curator of the secret/sacred collection at the South Australian Museum, also sees Aboriginal claims on these objects in this productive (over-productive?) way. This is partly because he emphasises restriction (of non-Aboriginal access to sacred objects) rather than loss (when non-Aboriginal collectors have their Aboriginal sacred objects taken away). In his article 'Aboriginal people and museums' (subtitled 'restricting access to increase it') Anderson describes the measures the South Australian Museum has taken to deal with Aboriginal claims on its collection. He thus offers us the kind of paradox we saw earlier in relation to the repatriation of human remains, involving a closed-yet-open structure from which both parties could benefit.[21] The South Australian Museum (SAM) has about 3000 sacred objects from Central Australia in its collection, most of which were donated to or purchased by the museum during the 1930s. By the 1960s, like other Australian museums with sacred objects, SAM, consulting with Aboriginal communities, had already removed this material from public display, securing its secrecy, its closure, its obscurity. By the early 1980s, however, SAM developed a programme of rehousing and safe storage of these objects, classifying and annotating them in dialogue with relevant Aboriginal communities. This process secured the closure of these objects on the one hand and animated them on the other, bringing Aboriginal voices back to objects which might previously have been collected with (in Griffiths' words) 'disdain for native informants'. So a kind of closed-yet-open structure emerges that, in Anderson's account, acts as 'a prelude to entering into discussions with elders about claims for return'.[22]

Anderson notes that very few cases of repatriation during the 1970s and early 1980s were successful. He speaks of 'the failure of the returns' at this point, mostly due to the apparent irreconcilability of the two parties: 'the problem was that what the Aborigines were asking opposed the basic premise of museums: collecting and keeping. Museums couldn't reconcile Aboriginal interests in items in their collections with their own brief as keepers of the cultural heritage'.[23] By contrast, Anderson sees his own museum as sufficiently animated by 'Aboriginal interests' such that repatriation becomes a key moment in the museum's life-cycle. Some of the gains he lists are well within the framework of the 'museum system' as a colonial force: improved documentation of objects already in the collection and an increase in the size of the collection when new objects are given to the museum for safe-keeping.[24] Other gains are more postcolonial: the freeing-up of previously restricted (mute, obscure) material for exhibition and research, and the sanctioning of the museum's role by Aboriginal communities which makes the museum 'much more viable and defensible politically'.[25] For Mulvaney and Murray, repatriation had produced loss, taking objects out of the 'museum system' and into muteness and obscurity. For Anderson, however, repatriation has not only animated those objects but renewed the 'museum system' itself. So perhaps a little repatriation in the right places is enough to unsettle the 'museum system' (sending it scurrying after its self-image, to shake off its new-found 'marginality'). Or, and this is just as likely, perhaps a little repatriation in the right places is enough to keep the whole thing together.[26]

Anderson's paradox, that restricted access produces increased access, makes him characterise Aboriginal claims over collected objects in exactly the opposite way to Tim Murray:

> What does 'access' really mean? It is my view that if museums stop focusing on issues of ownership and recognize instead a plurality of interests and rights in our material we may lose a few items through restitution and repatriation claims, but may also produce better and more appropriate access, we maximize usage of our collections, produce better exhibitions, increased documentation, and so on. 'Access' is thus in this sense redefined as being based on multiple and outward-looking rights to objects as opposed only to singular and 'inside' museum rights.[27]

Let us note just how different this response is to Murray's. Murray characterises Aboriginal claims over sacred objects as singular ('one strategy'), thereby compromising the apparent pluralism and open-ness of archaeology. But Anderson sees such claims as introducing plurality into the singularity of the 'museum system', in which case Aboriginal people are given rather than denied the 'democratic' coding. Anderson makes a point of saying that the renewed museum has turned its focus from the objects to the people themselves, a focus that makes these previously 'mute' relics speak as they had not

spoken before. Access means first and foremost Aboriginal access:
'Aboriginal elders were using sacred objects as a kind of social
currency . . . The difference is that they used the fact of our return
of objects (or rather our discussion making return a possibility) to
establish an ongoing relationship that allowed for joint and
interactive social relations'.[28] So the museum's sacred objects, and
Aboriginal claims made on them, come to provide the means by
which sociality is produced. Anderson's remarks move from the
objects' use-value to their exchange-value in a social system—where
Aboriginal claimants form a productive 'social relationship' with
the museum, visiting regularly, using the museum more than non-
Aboriginal researchers, handling their sacred objects.[29] This is a
Durkheimian point, that the sacred is a socialising force—so much
so in this account that the 'Aboriginal system' and the 'museum
system' are seamlessly woven together. The South Australian
Museum thus becomes emblematic in much the same way as
Mungo Lady, in that it stands as a 'sign' of reconciliation at its most
untroubled and benign. Anderson closes one of his articles on
SAM's new restricted openness with these remarks:

> Finally, at the most general level, we have the impression that
> Aboriginal people, instead of finding the museum to be an anony-
> mous alien institution, think of it as a knowing and benevolent en-
> vironment—the only place where they can see familiar things in the
> midst of urban white strangeness and anonymity.[30]

What has happened to the uncanny here? For non-Aboriginal
Australians, Aboriginal claims on property and objects can make
what is familiar seem unfamiliar—what is 'ours' is also 'theirs': our
home is also unhomely. But this passage puts an end to the uncanny
by turning it on its head. The South Australian Museum becomes a
home in the midst of unhomeliness for Aboriginal people, a position
of 'smiles' rather than 'worries'. The museum imagines itself as a
place where Aboriginal people can become familiar with themselves, as if the effects of dispossession are all around them, but no
longer here. The strange thing about this passage, then, is that
after the postcolonial event of responding to Aboriginal claims—
a modern event which impacts most directly on metropolitan

collections—the museum is able to displace itself into a precolonial imaginary. In effect, the South Australian Museum is imagined as a sacred site in the midst of the profane.

Anderson has also engineered the return of some of the museum's secret/sacred collection to Aboriginal claimants. He gives us a detailed account of his role in repatriation in the documentary *Sacred Journey* (1996), directed by Jim Roberts. In fact, the documentary charts a particular stage in the long process of repatriation, although it is actually a kind of interlude to it. Anderson begins by noting that the senior Aboriginal man who was meant to receive these sacred objects has since died, requiring him to 'start all over again'. His job now is to take a suitcase containing photographs of those sacred objects to 'another lot of men' with whom, at least in the narrative frame of the documentary, he has yet to meet. This narrative frame is broken up by several digressions involving claims about the role of the South Australian Museum, claims about the power of Aboriginal sacred objects, and an account of Anderson's credentials and family background. We can deal with these digressions one by one, because each of them speaks directly to the nature of this particular repatriation.

Anderson notes that repatriation is fraught with problems: there are museum colleagues who think 'I shouldn't be giving *anything* back' (his emphasis) on the one hand, and Aboriginal people who 'think it's taking too long' on the other. His view of repatriation is quite different to Murray's in that he recognises Aboriginal people as a privileged group 'to whom these objects are more significant than anybody else': these objects are not for 'all of us'. But he recognises them as a privileged group only in order to keep the 'museum system' together, to give it its desired completeness: 'only now are we beginning to recognise that the meaning of objects can't be fully known without that Aboriginal perspective'. We have already made this point: that repatriation may well unsettle the 'museum system', but it may also work to renew it and to re-establish its force. This force is consolidated through its own privileged role as the custodian of sacred objects which are invested with immense power. A number of people in the documentary testify to this power. Anderson himself says that the sacred objects are 'like compressed chunks of meaning and of power and of knowledge about the entire cosmos and how people fit into it'. Anthropologist Dick Kimber says that these sacred objects are 'the essence' of landscape and being, and of 'every other person of affiliation to that object'. Douglas Baker, chairman of the Pitjantjatjara Council, says: 'These sacred objects are the sacred stories of Australia, and we're looking after Australia'. What is interesting about these claims is that they give these sacred objects a broad reach, an extended sphere of influence, whereby the privileged group (the proper Aboriginal recipients) now extends outwards to become the nation itself. In this respect, Anderson sees repatriation as 'forging new links between Aboriginal people and mainstream Australia'. We can remember that, for Tim Murray, archaeology was the privileged group that looked after sacred objects in the interests of the nation, a position which was diminished by 'improper' Aboriginal intervention. Here, it is the other way around: Aboriginal people in full possession of their objects do not diminish the nation, they preserve it: 'all of us' are 'affiliated'.

But it is never easy to reconcile the interests of a privileged (let us say: 'marginal') group with the 'mainstream' interests of the nation. The willingness to equate these sacred objects with 'Australia' is always compromised by the need to retain their singularity, their specialness and exclusivity. So Dick Kimber tells us that SAM's collection is 'like an atomic bomb waiting to go off if the wrong people deal with it'. In this context it is important for the museum to make sure it is always doing the right thing; it is obliged to turn itself over to the 'Aboriginal system', at least to a degree. Anderson's account of his family background is precisely designed to do just this: to turn himself over to the 'Aboriginal system'. He was raised in West Virginia, in a place which, he says, was 'about 60 per cent black'. He played drums in a rhythm and blues band (photographs of black American musicians are shown at this point) and had black friends. For a short time he worked in a coal mine where, he says, 'you go in white and you come out black'. In Australia he works as an anthropologist in northern Queensland, and is touched by the power of the sacred ('It catches up with you'). He emphasises how long it took to become familiar with the 'Aboriginal system': 'It took me ages to learn the ropes'. Finally, he is experienced enough to deliver sacred objects to Central Australian Aboriginal people. Carrying the photographs of sacred objects in a suitcase, he drives for three days, eschewing civilisation, camping out in the bush rather than booking into hotels: 'I have to be *so* careful or else big trouble' (his emphasis). We join Anderson by his campfire one night when he reflects again upon the power of sacred objects, including the (photographs of) sacred objects he is delivering. He is especially concerned with the transference of sacred power from the objects to the courier:

> the things that are used to carry them, that they're wrapped in, the people that carry them, all of these things the power transfers to them . . . When I brought the objects back and the men saw me inter-acting with them, *it was as though I became a sacred object myself*, and the men sometimes rubbed me to gain the power that they saw that was there.[31]

Is this an example of the 'museum system' turning itself over to the 'Aboriginal system'? Or is it the other way around? The problem with so easily reconciling these two otherwise distinct things is that one can never tell which is pre-occupied by which. Nevertheless we can say that, in this telling of the story at least, it is Anderson rather than Central Australian Aboriginal people who benefits from the power of the sacred. This is partly due to his own new 'affiliations': repatriation provides him with a set of 'social relationships' he never previously had. But it is a strange predicament indeed to see a museum curator actually imagining (without a trace of irony) that he embodies the power of sacred objects!

We can thus recall the opening of this chapter, which looked at Tom Griffiths' account of what it was like to deliver sacred objects to the Museum of Victoria: how animated it made him feel, and yet how abject he became through his implication in a belated colonial process. Christopher Anderson drives his vehicle the other way: not back to the museum, but away from it (but how far?). He therefore never experiences Griffiths' abjection. The Weberian question that Griffiths had asked—'Was I participating in the dispossession of a people and the disenchantment of the world?'—would be completely foreign to him. Anderson imagines the 'museum system' to be so transformed that he cannot share this worry. As we have noted, he is driving the other way: towards *enchantment*, not disenchantment. But is he enchanted by the role he plays in enabling Aboriginal people to repossess their objects? Or in the power that role bestows upon him as the museum's curator, who is drawn to the 'Aboriginal system' but who comports himself in such a way that it is drawn back to him in turn ('the men sometimes rubbed me in order to gain the power they saw there')? In which case, has the transformation of the 'museum system' under postcolonial conditions made it into a completely different thing, or has it merely enhanced its charisma?

Authorising Sacredness

On Storytelling, Fiction and Uluru

W E HAVE ALREADY mentioned Emile Durkheim's concept of the 'totem', as a symbol through which a group can identity itself as a group: a symbol of corporateness (which is no doubt why it seems appropriate to modern business, as we've seen in Chapter 4). For Durkheim, of course, the most profound totem was society itself. His kind of sociology was premised on the view that the category of the individual, far from being characterised by self-fulfilment was, in fact, unfulfilled since he or she must be conscious of not belonging to a group. If one cannot identify oneself socially, one is in a condition defined by lack. The argument is still persuasive today: we can certainly account for social fragmentation and social unrest by saying that individualism (a capitalist democratic ideology which promises fulfilment but by no means delivers it) has come to replace a mode of identification structured through a shared sense of what 'society' actually is. One of the ironies of this condition is that it often carries with it the perception that a shared sense of the social is nevertheless retained by others, most notably, minority cultures. In a certain sense, to be 'Aboriginal' is, in many cases, to be able to lay claim to what others do not have: a (relatively) clear social identity, something akin to what is often called 'community'. Non-Aboriginal people, on the other hand, may figure themselves as lacking this kind of sociality. The point has been expressed in a British context in an article published in *New Formations* which wonders about the contemporary predicament in which whites have somehow come to see their whiteness as a drawback in this respect: 'there is a significant body of young, or youngish, white people in Britain's urban centres who don't feel they have an "ethnicity", or if they do, that it's not one they feel too good about'.[1] The historian Peter Cochrane has noticed a similar sensibility in contemporary Australia:

> Not so long ago, being ethnic was regarded, by some Australians, as an unfortunate condition that could only be cured by a move to a better country and a good dose of assimilation. Now things have changed. Being ethnic has a certain cachet, and being non-ethnic, meaning of old-Australian or Anglo-Celtic origin, has taken on negative connotations that figure in our comedy, film, politics and even literary awards . . . The 'non-ethnic' experience is, by implication, a negative, a lack, not much of an experience at all.[2]

Ethnicity is a social(ising) category which minority cultures can lay claim to but which whites, who already have a problematic relationship to other social categories such as class and gender, often have to forgo. In Australia's case, of course, ethnicity is a category which is mobilised through the agendas of multiculturalism: it is not just specific to Aboriginal people. Nevertheless, it is something this group has but certain others, white Australians or Anglo-Australians, for instance, may not have, or may have only in a secondary or belated sense (hence the new area of academic social inquiry: 'white studies'). By contrast, Aboriginal people put their ethnicity to use as a primary social category. It has a socially binding force to which even those other groups who may regard themselves as 'ethnic' may not be able to appeal. The overall point we are making here will recall our remarks about 'postcolonial racism' in previous chapters. Aboriginal people are a group of people who certainly have much less than others (less opportunities, worse health, etc.) but who also have what those others do not: their 'Aboriginality'. If non-Aboriginal people may be considered (or may, even, consider themselves) to lack this form of sociality, then something 'postcolonial' has clearly occurred. It was once the case, under the colonial regime, that the 'native'—the black Algerian in Frantz Fanon's classic study *Black Skin, White Masks* (1967), for example—felt the need to be white. Here, whiteness was something the black person did not have, but desired to have. The 'native' was construed as lacking from this point of view. Now, however, the scenario is, at least in part, reversed. Far from being construed as something to be gained, whiteness is a state of incompleteness. It is not ethnic *enough*, and it may try to compensate for this by imagining that it is surrounded with too much ethnicity or an ethnicity that has too much.

In his book *The Nervous System* (1994), expatriate Australian anthropologist, Michael Taussig, takes up Durkheim's notion of society as a totem which acts to complete an otherwise incomplete (that is, individualised) identity. Taussig does not seem to subscribe to the view that we are increasingly individualised—fragmented, dispersed, desocialised—under modern, Western conditions. Indeed, his view is that the totemic force of society (he calls it the 'State') is now more powerful than ever. Society, as many would probably agree, is something which has more power than the individual, which is why it is so important to be a part of it. Indeed, society is reified in this sense; Durkheim had talked about it as if it is quite distinct from individuals, as if it had acquired a power unto itself, as if it was a *deus ex machina*, something godlike, intangible and yet there. Taussig returns to Durkheim's descriptions of the socialising force of the sacred objects of Aboriginal people to express this sense of intangibility. Sacred objects are otherwise ordinary things (stones, pieces of wood, etc.) which are marked in certain ways. Those markings make them special, giving them totemic significance. The important point is that this significance always exceeds what it represents: the mark of a frog always represents something more than just a frog. The marks are both mimetic (certainly they show a frog) and abstract (they also show something more). In short, the signifier seems to exceed the signified: meaning exceeds representation. But this does not necessarily lead to the arbitrariness of the sign. For Durkheim, everyone participates in that 'excessive' meaning: the very fact of its excess produces socialisation. In other words, a sacred object exists both to represent something in the world (a frog, for instance) and also at the same time to articulate something far less tangible but more directly relevant and involving, namely, the fact of one's socialisation. Sacredness lies in this dual activity: it makes an ordinary thing extraordinary, and in allowing everyone to participate in or partake of that extraordinariness it produces sociality.

But how is this intangible thing authorised? In fact, much like Stephen Muecke in his work with Paddy Roe, Taussig depends for his account—for his rejection of the modern arbitrariness of the sign—on a 'traditionalist' view of Aboriginal authority. He turns to the early Australian anthropological work of Walter Baldwin Spencer and Frank Gillen to outline his points; and here, indeed, the authority of these anthropologists comes actually to stand for the Aboriginal authorisation of sacredness. Taussig takes the descriptions these anthropologists provide as true, in a process which actually removes Aboriginal people, who never actually speak in these early descriptive accounts, from the equation, rendering them mute. At one point in his book, Taussig says that he had wanted to reproduce 'Spencer and Gillen's drawing of the frog totem', but a colleague, Professor Annette Hamilton, an anthropologist from Macquarie University in Sydney, 'tells me that to reproduce the illustration would be considered sacrilege by Aboriginal people'.[3] It is not entirely out of the ordinary to suggest that the reproduction of a drawing of a sacred thing made by two anthropologists (long ago) would be viewed by Aboriginal people (these days) as 'sacrilegious'. But it is worth noting that this point is made, not by Aboriginal people themselves who once again never seem to have been consulted, but by another anthropologist on their behalf: as if 'Aboriginal people' have become a unified category which can be invoked whenever necessary. The prohibition on the reproduction of the drawing, in other words, has more to do with anthropological authorisation than Aboriginal authorisation, a point which is by no means idiosyncratic to this particular case. It seems that Taussig's concept of 'Aboriginal authorisation' in its traditional mode—in relation to the sacred, at any rate—is only able to be imagined anthropologically. He has performed 'Aboriginal authorisation' in this way, in order to suggest that a sacred image is still pristinely exclusive, as if tradition survives intact. And yet this performance has exactly the opposite effect. It shows that tradition can only become present today as a lack or an absence: a prohibition underwritten by a macro-ethnicity ('Aboriginal people') which is itself an entirely modern category. This may very well be an (albeit benign, even romantic) instance of the kind of compensatory mechanism described above: where one comes to imagine that one is surrounded by an ethnicity that is all too coherent—so coherent, in fact, that you need not bother to consult with it. Our point, however, is that this modern macro-ethnic category is invoked in order to preserve 'tradition' intact but only as something which can no longer be seen. And all this through an (un)authorised anthropological prohibition.

For contemporary Kooris, Murris and so on, ethnicity may not be quite so coherent as the modern category 'Aboriginal people' would suggest. We have already seen this in the case of Coronation Hill: to claim a site as sacred can throw up divisions or differences in a local community even as it enables coherence under the 'totem' of the social. The category of ethnicity may be similarly disturbed, even while it is appealed to, and non-Aboriginal Australians who themselves lack this category are often quick to exploit such disturbances, compensating for their own under-ethnicised condition in exactly the opposite way to what we had outlined above (as in: 'Aboriginal people are no more unified than we are'). We have no argument with Taussig's overall claim, following Durkheim, that under modern conditions the sacred, along with related concepts such as the taboo and the fetish, 'are redeemed and come alive with new intensity'.[4] This is precisely one of the features which comes to make Australia 'postcolonial' and it is a central topic in our book. Nevertheless, it does seem more true nowadays to say that a sacred object—or more particularly in our case, a sacred site—can produce both socialisation and difference, even amongst Aboriginal people themselves. This results, in part, because the sacred under modern conditions simply cannot remain intangible, exclusive, prohibited and absent: something must be said about it. The call—and often, the pressure—to speak about the sacred may very well compromise its intangibility and the kind of socialising force this intangibility may once have had. This is the point we want to elaborate at the beginning of this chapter: that the totemic function of the sacred (its ability to produce socialisation under the sign of 'Aboriginal people') is both undeniable and problematic because *it is an intangible thing that nevertheless must be talked about.*

It is, of course, because sacred objects and sites have been talked about so often and in so many contexts (not just anthropological contexts) that prohibitions on sacredness, which would preserve its exclusivity, have so frequently been broken. The usual way of resolving these transgressions is to draw a distinction between 'public' narratives about the sacred, and 'secret' or 'private' narratives. Decisions are made which align some narratives with the former category, and some with the latter. But are those decisions themselves 'public' in the sense that everyone involved is consulted and gives their agreement to them? Or might some groups —or even, some individuals—under certain conditions transgress these distinctions, speaking about sacredness in an 'unauthorised' way, for example? These are issues discussed by the late Eric Michaels in his work on Aboriginal film and televsion, and by Marcia Langton on her book *'Well, I Heard it on the Radio and I Saw it on the Television . . .'* (1993): they both advise a set of 'protocols' which non-Aboriginal people in particular could observe when engaging with Aboriginal narratives which may be secret. It is worth saying that Michaels especially built his concept of authorisation around a notion of the 'traditional' Aboriginal community; Aboriginal relations to television, for example, were seen as a series of negotiations made by a traditional community with a modern technology, mostly in order to preserve secrecy (traditional) from the onslaught of publicity (the modern: that is, television). In this context, the distinction between privacy and publicity can appear fairly clear-cut. But in other contexts, this may not be so. The problem is raised in the field of fiction, for example, a genre of writing which tends to confuse the distinctions between the public and the private or secret. Fiction is a form of writing which circulates in the public domain but is usually read privately. It is also written privately; it is not generally a collaborative or community-based form of cultural production. In fact, it can flourish by cutting its ties with community altogether. We have already noted that Bataille and the College of Sociology regarded fiction—the novel, at least—as something which thus stands *against* sacredness through its individualised, heretical mode of being-in-the-world. It therefore retains an 'unauthorised' character, consistent with its ambivalent relationship to truth. Moreover, fiction has often taken as its agenda the revelation of private or secret material; it is by its very nature a transgressive medium in this respect.

It is not surprising, then, to see anthropologists commenting that Aboriginal people, meaning traditional Aboriginal people, had no concept of fiction. Eric Michaels has made this point; and Stephen Muecke elaborates on it in his book *Textual Spaces*:

> Aboriginal societies . . . do not recognise a category 'fiction' . . . Stories are all true to the extent that the discourse is correctly produced within the cultural apparatuses which make it possible. Among the Aborigines of Broome there is no metalinguistic category 'fiction'. Stories are either true . . . or of the Dreaming. And to say they are true means to say that you were there, or you knew someone who was who gave you the story; or its validity as a collective production is amply demonstrable if the listener is referred to someone who is the uncle of the main character in the story, and so on.[5]

This account places its emphasis on sociality and ethnicity as a frame for Aboriginal narrative: it is a 'collective production' which relies on Aboriginal presence ('you were there . . .'). This is why it is difficult to imagine that Aboriginal people had a category of 'fiction'. Fiction does not rely on presence at all. One need not have been 'there' at the site of fiction; there is no necessary or authentic connection between fiction (signifier) and place (signified). So fiction need not depend upon 'presence', nor need it be bound to place—two features which would seem to disqualify it from the realm of Aboriginal storytelling. In this sense, fiction would seem to have been a 'luxury' that traditional Aboriginal communities did without. Muecke's account not only stresses the 'collective' or communal production of Aboriginal narratives, but also the 'correct' production: 'true stories' are always authorised. But fiction is again problematic here, as we have already noted. It is not that fiction is anti-authoritarian; rather, it is a genre of writing which turns the concept of 'authority' into a problem, not least because—since it is often so severed from place, community and presence—the 'cultural apparatuses which make it possible' can be difficult to determine.

In one of his chapters, Muecke reads a narrative by Paddy Roe, an Aboriginal elder from Broome, which he titles 'The children's country'. The narrative is spoken by Roe to his children, and concerns a claim for land which is connected to sacredness.

Muecke's reading deals mostly with the way in which Roe's narrative enacts the kind of authorisation needed to enable him to say what he says, as an Aboriginal elder. The narrative is seen as primarily ethical or pedagogical, in that it works to 'orient the subject [the listening subjects—Paddy Roe's children—as well as the speaking subject, Roe himself] in discourse'.[6] It 'provides points of insertion for listening subjects [the children] who may want to take up his story and tell it again'.[7] But Muecke's emphasis on the ethical features of the narrative, which place the speaker and the listeners in a particular relation to one another—a relation of presence, a direct relationship—is at the expense of attending to what the narrative is actually about. As Muecke puts it: 'I have subsumed the referential or informative function of language under the instructional, because information is indifferent to subject positions, at least when it is idle'.[8] In our view, this distinction between a process of instruction which works actively on the speaker and the listeners, and the 'idle' aspect of what is actually being conveyed, is a false one. Muecke does at one point draw attention to the 'informative' aspect of Roe's narrative when he says that it 'takes up the issue of land rights, but skirts around it in an indirect manner'.[9] So the 'informative' aspect of Roe's narrative is not 'idle' so much as 'indirect', even when the narrative itself is offered directly to a family group, a group of children. Of course, this narrative is by no means so clearly directed, since it is, after all, recorded by a visiting scholar (Muecke) and then included in a book which is marketed globally with a recommendation on the back cover from an American humanities academic. The narrative, spoken directly by Roe to his children, will thus also be received 'indirectly' by other readers, including us, who may likewise find 'points of insertion' for themselves in what is being said and may even (although no doubt in quite different ways to Paddy Roe's children) 'want to take up his story and tell it again'. The narrative, in other words, has been put into the public domain, and is thus available for comment from people well outside its closed community circle. In this much less secure, less exclusive context—which cuts across the bond between the story and its immediate audience (another version of signifier and signified)—it may thus not be surprising that the narrative 'skirts around' what it has to say about sacredness 'in an indirect manner'.

So what *does* this narrative have to say about sacredness? It is possible to suggest, in fact, that Paddy Roe takes up this issue of what to say about sacredness, and talks about it directly. His country around Broome in north-west Western Australia is a highly publicised and attractive tourist destination. Part of the problem when making special claims for land traversed by groups of people from other parts of Australia and other parts of the world involves trying to distinguish Aboriginal interests from the interests of others: to make what is Aboriginal distinctive or 'different'. But this means that sacredness (as one of the indicators of that 'difference') has to be spoken about, in which case it ceases to be the intangible thing it may once have been. In Paddy Roe's account, this sense of the intangibility of the sacred is evoked as a means of talking about what the land was like before tourism, before people came from elsewhere and the bond between Aboriginal people and place was disrupted. In this precolonial time, the sacred was intangible because there was simply no need to speak (about) it:

> we never say, 'You come from that part of the country, you come from that part of the country', no, we never say those sorta things—
> all the people is all same to us—
> because they know their boundary, they go back—
> we know—
> we know our old people's boundary too they all go back to each boundary—[10]

Under these traditional (precolonial, pre-tourism) conditions, then, everyone knows their 'boundaries': there is no transgression, and thus there is no need for prohibitions. Because everyone knows about their 'boundaries'—and we take sacred sites to be a feature of this knowledge—there is no need to put it into 'language', meaning the particular Aboriginal language of Roe's community. Roe insists on this point in his narrative:

> but language got nothing to do—
> no, language got NOTHING to do—
> with the country—[11]

This insistence on a precolonial intangibility, however, is made in the context of some remarks about what conditions are like now, rather than then. Under the pressures of colonialism and tourism, boundaries have since become blurred; an Aboriginal claim for land competes with other claims. A local place is put to use by people from elsewhere who have no idea where those original boundaries might be, who do not always 'go back' to their own original places, and who in any case bring quite different languages to bear upon the subject:

> ANY language can live—
> today—
> English, Japanese, Chinese, we all friend—
> we all living together now—
> we can't say where they come from—[12]

Once everyone knew about their 'boundaries', but now the place is in a kind of unbounded condition. It was once the case that 'we never say', that is, never needed to say, where people came from; but now 'we *can't* say'. A loss of authorisation seems to have occurred here, and it seems to produce a self-consciousness about 'language' in this narrative: that there are other available languages at work in this place, that 'today young generation' (the children to whom the narrative is directed, as well as others) may not have Roe's traditional language, and so on. Language is stretched as a result (Roe uses a 'bridging' form of Aboriginal English rather his local Nyigina language), to become more inclusive, not just in terms of the need to address a wider, less socialised community (the younger generation of Aboriginal children, readers from elsewhere, tourists), but also in the sense that *language must now include the sacred.* This means that things which were previously unarticulated in language must now be spoken: something (new) must be said. In the context of so many languages and such unboundedness, how can a particular kind of sociality, an Aboriginal kind of sociality, be recovered? The problem is tied, in part, to a recovery of privacy from the glare of a marauding public, even though the fact that what is private must still be articulated to other people/readers always compromises this point. Paddy Roe works out the recovery of something sacred by drawing a distinction between the 'top soil'—which is traversed by tourists and others, and is public and unbounded and transgressive in this sense—and the 'bottom soil', which is more secretive, secure and exclusive:

> but the top soil is belongs to ANYbody can walk—
> walk around, camp, ANYwhere, we can't tell-im he got no right to
> be there—
> if he got right to camp because the top soil is belongs to him—
> but the bottom, the bottom soil, the bottom soil that's belongs to my
> family, family trustees, family group—
> family trustees—[13]

This wonderful distinction—given a kind of legal sanction through the phrase 'family trustees'—certainly works to conceal what is Aboriginal from the gaze of a modern, marauding world. In a sense, this distinction between the private and the public is consistent with a foundational point made by Durkheim in his attempt to make a case for the exclusivity of the sacred, that the sacred must always be separated from the 'profane': 'The sacred thing', he says, 'is *par excellence* that which the profane should not touch'.[14] The former is usually seen as authorised, traditional and religious, while the latter is seen as secular, modern and transgressive, and these things would seem always to remain distinct from each other. This is a powerful binary and it certainly underwrites the recovery of Aboriginal authority as a traditional force. The articulation of an intimate bond to place (which authority depends upon) results in the 'burial' of what is Aboriginal underground, in the 'bottom soil': Western tourists have only the surface but Aboriginal people have depth. But does that mean that the surface, the land itself, is lost for Aboriginal people in this equation? What is to be gained by removing the sacred in this way from a surface which is coded as modern and secular through its association with marauding tourists, with readers from elsewhere, with globalisation? Does it turn what is specifically Aboriginal into a kind of absence, like the drawing of the frog totem that Michael Taussig had declined to reproduce? It is difficult not to register an ambivalence about this strategy of disentangling the Aboriginal from the modern, evocative as Paddy Roe's narrative may be. Does this 'burial' (and this must be only the most tentative of questions) inevitably work to restrain sacredness as a kind of relic? Or does it endow sacredness (as an 'underground' expression of that intimate bond to place) with latent potential? Is this a productive way of identifying what belongs to Aboriginal people, what can be authorised by Aboriginal people, in the modern world? The distinction between the 'top soil' and the 'bottom soil' is, anyway, compromised even as it is made, since it produces what is Aboriginal as something which is hidden-for-all-to-see: a secret which is shared, as all secrets must inevitably be: closed yet open.

The classic essay 'The Storyteller' (1936) by the German critic Walter Benjamin can help us think about what is at stake when we move from an authorising narrative, such as Paddy Roe's, to the kind of modern Aboriginal fiction we find with, say, Sam Watson's *The Kadaitcha Sung* (1990), a novel that, as we noted in an earlier chapter, Stephen Muecke had found 'virtually unreadable'. For Benjamin, the storyteller worked primarily in an oral tradition. He gave 'counsel' to his listeners; he was bound to place; he was 'corporeal'; he had presence. He transmitted something 'useful' from which his listeners could benefit; he was wise and authorising; and he spoke from a lifetime's experience. He involved his listeners—who, it is assumed, do not have what he has; who lack—in a direct relationship with himself. In this sense, Paddy Roe is a storyteller. Indeed, senior Aboriginal men are often figured in this way, as storytellers in Benjamin's sense of the term. The novelist, by contrast, can claim neither the storyteller's wisdom and authority, nor the direct relationship he has to his listeners. For Benjamin, in fact, the rise of the novel coincides exactly with the decline of the storyteller:

> The earliest symptom of a process whose end is the decline of story-telling is the rise of the novel at the beginning of modern times . . . *The novelist has isolated himself*. The birthplace of the novel is the solitary individual, who is no longer able to express himself by giving examples of his most important concerns, is himself uncounselled, and cannot counsel others.[15]

The novel, equated with the modern world, is imagined only as a condition of loss: the loss of orality, tradition, authority, all the things regarded as central to the craft of Aboriginal storytelling. Melbourne-based author, Arnold Zable, gives expression to this view when he says the following about Aboriginal stockman Herb Wharton's book *Where Ya' Been, Mate* (1996):

> As I finished [it], the fiendish thought came to me: what if we were to rip out the electric cords from their sockets and black out the televisions and personal computers that glow in the rooms of suburbia. For just a few weeks, mind you. Then we would probably discover an 'illiteracy' of a different kind: our increasing inability to spin a simple yarn, eye to eye, about realities that transcend our electronic aids. Ah, then we would have to turn to our Herb Whartons for retraining in the most ancient of communicating arts: storytelling.[16]

The 'we' in this passage are the moderns: 'us'. Zable's remarks return to the kind of point we (the authors . . .) had outlined at the beginning of this chapter: that modern people, modern non-Aboriginal people it is surely implied, no longer possess the craft of storytelling. Storytelling is taken as a form of social cohesion since it 'communicates'; but under modern conditions 'we' are seen as atomised and isolated from each other, 'illiterate' and untrained in these respects, enslaved to the otherwise gratuitous 'luxuries' of television and the World-Wide Web. This is certainly an emotive way of imagining the modern world, both nostalgic (about the past) and abject (about the present). Nevertheless, it helps to make the point that Aboriginal narratives are so often seen as a form of 'storytelling' that the modern world, with its television and its computers—and its novels—has disavowed.

In the light of these remarks, what happens when an Aboriginal man writes a novel about a sacred site? Should we see this simply as an enactment of this man's loss of authority and sense of tradition in the context of a modern world? Can a modern novel, as it comes inevitably to articulate the arbitrariness of the sign, have nothing definite to say about sacredness at all? Sam Watson's novel *The Kadaitcha Sung* is based around Uluru, probably the most spectacular sacred site in the world. But Watson comes from Brisbane and has no direct connection to the Aboriginal communities—the Pitjantjatjara—who help to look after Uluru and continue to tell its stories. In an obvious sense, this does restrict his authority. But it also opens up new possibilities and potentials which fiction, precisely because of its unbounded relationship to place and its ambivalence towards authority, is able to exploit.

The Kadaitcha Sung is an exhilarating yet disturbing novel which imagines a primordial Aboriginal battle working itself out in late colonial or postcolonial times. The battle is over the theft of a sacred object, the Kundri stone. White colonials—judges and policemen especially—are presented as cruel and brutal along the way, but the battle itself is between the evil kadaitcha man who covets the stone, Booka Roth, and his brother's kadaitcha child, Tommy Gubba. The identification of these characters as kadaitchas gives them a certain traditionality: kadaitcha men are senior Aboriginal magic men or (to draw on the title of A. P. Elkin's famous book) 'Aboriginal men of high degree', dealing out pay-backs or revenge on transgressors who break the Law.[17] But these kadaitchas are also modern/colonial, marauding figures who themselves have a transgressive function. In an interview titled 'Liberty taken with the legends', Watson has remarked: 'I've given them [the kadaitcha men] a lot of powers they haven't been reported as having'.[18] We can see this in the novel's articulation of Aboriginal Law, since the extra powers Watson ascribes to the kadaitcha men in fact enable them to break the Law as much as they uphold it. Booka had (even before white colonisation) 'interfered in the sacred order of all things', as if that order had never been stable,[19] and the younger man, the hero Tommy Gubba, often upsets Aboriginal elders. Gubba has a white mother and is a hybrid figure, located in between 'two camps'.[20] His surname is a common Aboriginal word for a white person, a colloquial abbreviation of the word 'government'. Both preserving and unsettling the authority of his Aboriginal elders—many of whom express outright disapproval of him, not least because his concerns are mostly with a new generation of Aboriginal youth—he has a role to play that is very much like Cooloombrah in the story by Ray Kelly we looked at in Chapter 3. It would not be difficult to see him as a particular manifestation of an 'Aboriginal bureaucrat'.

Watson's novel is striking for its rendering of violence between colonials and Aboriginal people, and between Aboriginal people who transgress and Aboriginal people who are sent to avenge those transgressions. But it is also striking for its graphic and recurrent accounts of sexual perversions. In a sense, this is a novel that has 'everything': there is never a dull moment. What other Australian novel has so relentlessly presented us with so many scenes depicting acts of anal intercourse, for example—which reviewers politely neglect to mention? Senior Brisbane judges sodomise Aboriginal women; an Aboriginal man sodomises Stephen, a white English lecturer; Gubba's girlfriend actually wants to be sodomised; while Gubba himself fantasises erotically about his mother's underwear. Vivien Johnson has reported, in an article in the Sydney journal *Art & Text*, that she was 'surprised to discover that "gubba" actually came from an Aboriginal word meaning "white demon"—and shocked to learn its secondary meaning, "peeping tom"'.[21] Tommy Gubba certainly evokes these meanings through his behaviour in a novel which is saturated with sexual activity. Indeed, although *The Kadaitcha Sung* is about the recovery of a sacred object, at the same time it is a novel which revels in the profane: the ordinariness, and the extra-ordinariness, of sexual activity in particular. When he finally finds the sacred stone, Gubba almost immediately forgets about it, distracted by a couple routinely having sexual intercourse nearby—as if sacredness and profanity do touch each other, in spite of Durkheim's pronouncement. Of course, Durkheim was never content with clear distinctions. He had, in fact, noted that the necessary separation of the sacred from the profane 'cannot go so far as to make all communication between the two worlds impossible', but he had wanted to preserve this impossibility none the less: 'the mind irresistibly refuses to allow the two corresponding things to be confounded, or even to be merely put into contact with each other; *for such a promiscuity . . . would contradict too violently the dissociation of these ideas in the mind*'.[22] *The Kadaitcha Sung* is a 'promiscuous' novel in precisely this sense. It knows that the sexual acts it documents are both mundane and perverse, yet it puts them right alongside its evocation of Aboriginal sacredness. Indeed, Tommy Gubba at one point even inserts the sacred stone 'into his scrotal sac': 'Now he would have three balls for a couple of days',[23] the novel jokes, as it quite literally places the sacred and the profane 'violently' into proximity with each other.

This novel works in quite the opposite way to Paddy Roe's narrative, then, in that far from trying to disentangle the sacred from the profane it actually places them in a highly 'promiscuous' relationship with one another. The fact that the sacred stone comes from Uluru may well account for this. Uluru is taken in the novel as a kind of meta-sacred site which reaches right across the nation. *The Kadaitcha Sung* is therefore a 'national fiction', playing out both a mythical and a modern battle for the nation's soul. The significance of the sacred stone even reaches across to Africa in this novel, as if its power recognises almost no boundaries at all. But Uluru stands at the centre of all this, drawing characters into its frame no matter how far away they may be. The unbounded potential of Uluru is taken as empowering in the novel, producing a set of special effects which are mobilised to underwrite the nation's modern condition. Everyone comes under its influence: to recall Rosa Praed's description of the bunyip in the story we examined in Chapter 2, it emanates its aura across Australia, and 'deals out promiscuously benefits and calamities from the same hand'. Let us pause (again) over that word 'promiscuous'. As Broome was for Paddy Roe, of course, so Uluru is itself a globalised, traversed site. It is one of Australia's most popular tourist destinations, and many of those tourists make a point of climbing over the Rock's surface. Its unbounded potential empowers it in one sense but makes it vulnerable in another, since it becomes difficult to regulate tourist interests in the Rock. In Paddy Roe's words, 'we can't say where they came from': so many people from so many different places come to Uluru to bask in its aura. The sense that Uluru touches so many people, and that so many people come to touch Uluru, makes it much more inclusive than exclusive. It is certainly not exclusive to Aboriginal people, nor is it immune from adaptation by those marauding tourists who come under its spell. Julie Marcus has noted how New Age groups in the United States endow Uluru with special powers which radiate outwards across the globe, in a way that (broadly speaking) is not entirely dissimilar to its representation in Watson's novel.[24] More recently, Barry Hill, in his meticulously researched book on Uluru, has commented on the problem of visitors and tourists, New Agers in particular, both speaking against promiscuity and recognising the impossibility of preventing it: '*Sometimes it means saying "no" to love* . . . [But] how can one control what the spiritually oriented person thinks and feels when they come to the Rock?'[25] There is, then, a sense that the Rock is 'open' to a range of appropriations from its many visitors simply because it is what it is—and that this openness is difficult to control even when the Rock is touched (and touches in return) out of love. This is what might lead us to characterise Uluru as a promiscuous sacred site.

Can the sacredness of Uluru be disentangled from all this love? Barry Hill's book begins with one of the traditional Aboriginal owners of Uluru, Tony Tjamiwa, claiming that Bill Harney, bushman and author of a popular guide to the Rock first published back in 1964, 'didn't know anything' because he was 'not from around here'.[26] Hill's book is an attempt to build a more informed and comprehensively 'postcolonial' view of Uluru, in the wake of Harney's earlier perceptions. It is concerned with developing an appropriate set of knowledges about Uluru which properly respond to what the local traditional Aboriginal owners, the Anangu, have to say. But it also recognises that Uluru is an 'open' place, and that other groups make claims upon it. Under the direction of the Hawke Labor government in 1985, title to Uluru—previously known only as Ayers Rock (that is, without 'ethnicity')—was transferred to the Anangu on the understanding that the Rock and its surroundings be managed jointly by them and by the National Park authorities. This transfer, heatedly objected to at the time by the Northern Territory government amongst others, enabled local Aboriginal people to gain a significant amount of control over Australia's most prominent natural icon and tourist attraction, control which by no means blocked the business of the tourism industry as many had feared. 'Joint management' is one way into a future condition of reconciliation. Barry Hill's chapter on 'sharing' between the Anangu, the Australian Nature Conservation Agency and tourist industry operators, however, documents some of the unsettlements which prevent this condition from being fully realised. Tim Rowse

was one of the authors of a commissioned study into joint management at Uluru, titled *Sharing the Park: Anangu Initiatives in Ayers
Rock Tourism* (1991). In a rewritten version of the concluding essay
published in 1992, Rowse speaks of the 'host' Anangu owners, and
of the various non-Anangu 'guests' who visit the Rock from elsewhere. In a very real sense, both 'hosts' and 'guests' share the Rock
but their entanglement ebbs and flows unevenly:

> The 'hosts' and 'guests' depicted in *Sharing the Park* are perhaps
> ironically labelled. Anangu 'hosts' want financial benefits from a
> mass tourism that they did not seek, and with which they do not now
> wish to interact. Consequently, there are thousands more non-
> Anangu 'guests' who would like to interact with their 'hosts'; and the
> more there are, the less likely such interaction is to occur, except for
> a very fortunate few. Meanwhile the tourist industry seems more
> geared . . . to a (non-interactive) confirmation of the pre-eminence of
> geological spectacle among the region's attractions: to savour the
> primeval landscape requires no 'hosting', not even a bus driver's
> interpretation.[27]

Rowse registers the unease some Anangu feel at losing control over
ever-increasing levels of mass tourism. His point is that the 'hosts'
must come to interact more fully with the 'guests' so that they might
each become more 'comprehensible' to each other. Rowse quotes
two other authors from *Sharing the Park* who suggest that the
'impersonal' nature of the relations between Anangu and tourists
hinders rather than benefits the former's self-determination,[28] and
that it is important to become entangled with those marauding
tourists even as the Anangu maintain their own distinctiveness. The
Rock is thus taken as simultaneously open (to tourists, to people
who are 'not from around here') and closed (there are exclusive,
prohibited sites on the Rock, as expressions of distinctively local
Aboriginal claims upon the place). But it is also acknowledged, in
Hill's book especially, that openness and closure, although they co-
exist, are not yet reconcilable to each other.

    Watson's novel might very well function as a 'guest' under this
logic, in the sense that it comes in the wake of Uluru's openness to
others, to those who are connected to it indirectly rather than

directly (that is, locally as owners or even as 'joint managers'). But it is also an Aboriginal novel and is able to play out its 'host' status at the same time, as if the distinction between the one and the other is now itself difficult to settle. The problem is that by playing host to the Rock, by using it as the source of a primordial yet pan-Aboriginal and thus modern form of power, the novel simply elaborates on rather than problematises the Rock's openness. It never mentions any local Aboriginal communities and it has no interest in the particularity of site claims on Uluru itself. Its task instead is to use the Rock as a symbol of Aboriginal power broadly speaking, which is then unleashed 'promiscuously' across the nation. So, as we have already noted, Watson's novel works in quite the opposite way to Paddy Roe's narrative. Whereas the latter gives a nuanced and restrained account of the location of Aboriginal sacredness in the modern world—underground, tucked away from the surface world of modernity and marauding tourism—Watson's novel is quite unrestrained: flagrant, excessive. We must make the point that this is perfectly consistent with the characteristics of fiction, as outlined above, and we should also note just how this point comes to contradict completely Benjamin's lament that 'the novelist has isolated himself'. Indeed, in the case of fiction it is quite the opposite: the novelist is not isolated *enough*! Fiction is not bound to place; it is 'open' in a range of ways (to influences from elsewhere, to interpretation by others, and so on), and it is thus ambivalent, if not downright disrespectful, about the roles of tradition and authority (roles ascribed to the 'storyteller') which are themselves much less open and unbound. The interview cited earlier, 'Liberty taken with the legends', makes a point along these lines when it locates that 'liberty' in the novel's generic identity as a popular horror-thriller. *The Kadaitcha Sung* is certainly an 'Aboriginal novel'; but the interviewer rightly notes that Watson's influences also 'range from the Book of Genesis to Greek mythology to Steven Spielberg to Steven [*sic*] King'.[29] Elsewhere, Watson has remarked that he was writing about 'Aboriginal power', but that he also wanted to reflect a social context involving people 'from a vast variety of backgrounds' who 'spoke many different tongues', which enabled him to keep 'an open mind' about other issues and other cultures.[30] So this is a novel which entangles its traditionality and its modernness; it is both specifically Aboriginal and open to a range of other formations which are 'not from around here'. This entanglement registers its own 'promiscuous' status as a novel which is touched by others and touches in return (directly, and indirectly; locally, nationally and, potentially at least, globally). But let us finally return to the novel's excesses. We must note that these, too, are consistent with its fictional status—and we must at least try to register a distinction between these features and Durkheim's point about the 'excessive' nature of the sacred thing. Something is sacred because its significance exceeds what it is. And for Durkheim, a sacred thing produces socialisation because everyone can participate in that excessive significance. Uluru is an example of a sacred thing whose significance exceeds what it is: it is so much more than just a 'rock' or a 'monolith'. But it is the excessive nature of this significance—the fact that Uluru can radiate out so far, that it can attract so many people from so many places—that in this case breaks through socialisation ('sharing') to prevent it from realising itself. Uluru has had an Aboriginal ethnicity imprinted upon it since 1985—but at the same time, it continues to remain 'open' and 'available'. Aboriginal fiction can participate in this dilemma, but it cannot resolve it.

Promiscuous Sacredness

On Women's Business, Publicity and Hindmarsh Island

WHEN THE amateur anthropologist Walter Arndt first encountered the Jawoyn 'Bula cult' in the area of Coronation Hill, his initial preoccupation was with verifying whether it was or was not a 'hoax'.[1] Arndt posed this question in the context of the science of Aboriginal sacredness: verification was needed in order for his account of this 'cult' to pass legitimately into the records of Australian anthropology. At stake was the reputation of an aspiring amateur anthropologist. In contemporary Australia, however, the verification of Aboriginal claims over the sacredness of country has taken on entirely different proportions. Aboriginal people who make public claims of this kind do so in the context of a competitive framework of multiple land-use. Legal provisions for the recognition of Aboriginal interests in land and Aboriginal prior occupation of the continent have meant that such claims, far from being ignored or confined to the pages of anthropological journals, have to be dealt with by a variety of institutions and organisations as a matter of course. In particular, such claims must enter the sphere of governmental and legal adjudication where they are once again subject to the pressures of proof of evidence. In order to verify it in these spheres, sacredness has to be talked about. But this requirement often seems entirely at odds with the structures of exclusivity which attend the Aboriginal sacred and which work to make it a special thing, a secret thing.

What happens when sites which are associated with secrecy enter into the public sphere of advocacy, policy and the law, as they must do when Aboriginal people seek to have such sites protected? Contemporary legal and policy provisions have, in fact, attempted to accommodate the protocols of secrecy associated with Aboriginal sacred sites. Land claim hearings regularly have what are called 'closed' sessions in which secret sacred evidence can be presented. Civil courts have ruled in favour of stopping information Aboriginal people consider to be secret from being published. Management strategies for land over which Aboriginal interests are recognised routinely include measures to ensure the exclusivity of sites which have secret sacred content: restricted on-the-ground access, locked registers of site information, and so on. Secrecy seems like a taken-for-granted category in these examples, which recognise it and treat it with respect. But it is equally true that Aboriginal claims to land that are framed by secrecy can produce specific worries about truth and validity—a scepticism, in other words— which troubles the provisions which postcolonial Australia has installed in order to recognise Aboriginal sacredness. We saw a form of this modern scepticism expressed in relation to the Coronation Hill claim where doubts were raised about the age of the belief, the actual location of Bula, and which Aboriginal people had the authority to speak for Bula's country. The response to Coronation Hill was a symptom of an emerging view that at least some Aboriginal claims are illegitimate because they are recent 'inventions' that respond not to the logic of tradition but to the logic of modernity. For those touched by scepticism, such claims are never only for the sacred but always also against development ('progress'), as if these two things are necessarily incommensurable with each other. For the sceptics, secrecy obscures (rather than secures) the validity of the sacred and suggests a possible future in which there might be endless unverifiable Aboriginal claims for it. Secrecy can be taken as a demonstration of how 'peculiar' traditional Aboriginal connections to sacredness once were, in that they were none of 'our' business. But a sceptical view of secrecy sees it in quite the opposite way: there is now no telling how the sacred might function to block the business of modern Australia.[2] So the protocols of secrecy which can be associated with Aboriginal sites are, on the one hand, recognised and accommodated, but on the other hand, they can allow uncertainty and anxiety to flourish. This chapter examines the fortunes which attend claims by Aboriginal people to have their secret sacred business recognised by the modern nation. What happens when the secret status of sites must be articulated in the public domain? Are the exclusivities associated with such sites sustained or compromised? What worries does the performance of secrecy in the public sphere produce for Aboriginal people, and for others?

We shall focus on two Aboriginal claims which have brought the issue of secrecy into the public sphere where it was fussed over and worried about in various ways: the Arrernte claims over sites near Alice Springs, and the Ngarrindjeri claims over sites on Hindmarsh Island, South Australia. In both of these examples claims were made by Aboriginal women to preserve their secret sacred women's business in the face of developments which placed those sites at risk. Both entailed lengthy public struggles over the legitimacy of those claims. Of course, the realm of secret sacred women's business has, in a certain sense, already been touched by scepticism. It was not until the 1970s, under the influence of what has come to be called 'feminist anthropology', that this aspect of Aboriginal life was more widely documented. Until then, women's business was assumed to play an ancillary role to the more important ritual life of men. So the anthropological verification of Aboriginal women's business came to be through the influence of a relatively new strand of the discipline, which actively advocated for the recognition of 'marginal' interests. For some, this entanglement of Aboriginal women's business and an avowedly reformist feminist anthropology has worked only to generate further doubts. Indeed, at times the public arbitrations associated with such claims pay as much attention to the validity of a 'special interest' branch of anthropology as they do to the claims themselves. Certainly, for South Australian journalist Chris Kenny, the claims by Ngarrindjeri women that Hindmarsh Island was a secret sacred site could not be disentangled from his view that the anthropologist who assisted them, Deane Fergie, had 'staked her career on confidential female traditions and gender exclusivity'.[3] Chris Kenny was one of a number of male contributors to a local magazine, the *Adelaide Review*, who used the opportunity the Hindmarsh Island affair gave them to pillory both Aboriginal women who claim sacredness and feminist anthropologists, as if these two groups could not be distinguished from one another. Emeritus Professor of History at the University of Adelaide, Austin Gough, saw feminist anthropology as an 'industry capable of generating dense clouds of mysticism and tendentious rhetoric',[4] a remark that rests far too easily with the stereotypical casting of women and Aboriginal people as irrational and secretive, yet cunning and interfering: obscuring rather than verifying. Gough tells us that the Hindmarsh Island affair has revealed 'what universities have known for some time: that it is very hard to cope with feminist anthropology'.[5] What can we say about this expression of anxiety? The confident invocation of 'what universities have known' rests uneasily with the strangely archaic view that feminism has been nothing but a bother to these modern institutions. But at the same time, this idiosyncratic remark does resonate with one feature of the larger concern which our own book has been charting: that the nation finds it 'very hard to cope' with Aboriginal claims upon it.

One might imagine that a site which is claimed as being both significant and secret is always an exclusive thing: only certain people know about it, sometimes its precise location is known only by a select few, and usually the specifics of its content are guarded. But in modern Australia a secret sacred site is never entirely exclusive or intangible. For the special status that secrecy confers upon a place to be understood—for it to confer the significance it is intended to—there needs to be at least some level of disclosure and some spread of information. In some cases, in fact, large numbers of people need to know that this is a secret place meant only for a few, in order to protect that place from inappropriate uses and visitations. Ensuring the exclusivity of a sacred site thus requires that its secret status be articulated to a broader audience. Indeed, the exclusivity of a secret site may actually depend upon casting a broad sphere of influence into which a wide range of people are drawn. We have made this point in earlier chapters: that as soon as claims are made for the recognition of a sacred site in a modern context, a certain amplification occurs which both secures that site's exclusivity and compromises it at the same time. This expansion of sacredness can certainly help to protect a site but it can produce risks as well. When a secret enters this enlarged system of recognition then there are pressures for it to be spoken about. The predisposition of the law and government towards proof through testimony itself produces pressures for secrets to be told, notwithstanding the protocols they have put in place. In the process, secrecy is performed to a broader and less predictable network of people, some of whom are affectionate towards Aboriginal secrecy and others who lose no time in giving their scepticism full expression. There is no telling how, where and by whom one's secrets may be received.

When Aboriginal groups make claims on the nation to recognise their secret sacred sites, they often adopt a strategy of partial disclosure: they might tell some groups and people about their secret stories but decline to tell others. Partial disclosure was certainly the initial strategy of the Arrernte women of Central Australia when they sought to protect the site they call Welatye-Therre from being lost under water as a result of the proposed construction of a recreation/flood mitigation dam near Alice Springs. In the early 1980s when the plans to build a dam were just emerging, the Arrernte women called upon the Northern Territory Sacred Site Protection Authority to record their site, under the condition that this information not be widely circulated. In calling upon this Authority the Arrernte women were willing to compromise the exclusivity of this site in order that it be recognised by the law. As the initial proposals to build a dam consolidated, however, the Arrernte women experienced their own scepticism about the law's ability to protect their site. They decided, somewhat reluctantly, that it may be necessary to let more people know about the significance of Welatye-Therre. So began the process of publicising their cause to a larger audience. Selected journalists were invited to the site and were told certain things about it. Arrernte women even allowed photographs of the site, and of one of the women 'cradling' a sacred stone which was stored there, to be taken and published in the print media. But while selected journalists had this site revealed to them, they were also told that there were things about this place that should continue to be kept secret. The media report produced

by this 'disclosure' told readers about the site only in order to tell
them that they could never *know* about that site: 'The dry Todd
River bed in Alice Springs conceals an ancient secret story of
violence and rape. Only Aboriginal eyes which know the Dreaming
can read and understand the story, laid out in rocky out crops in the
river bank'.[6] This 'disclosure' by Arrernte women was both a vague
revelation of its meaning and a performance of the site's secret
status in the public sphere. Their engagements with the public
domain at this point entailed negotiating between what could be
spoken and what should remain unspeakable—a negotiation which
then itself came to be the means by which others could come to
'know' the sacred.

This public performance of (partial) secrecy, far from keeping
this site as an exclusive thing, opened opportunities for others to
affiliate with it and the Arrernte women's cause. In the ongoing
struggle to protect the site through their support group, the
Welatye-Therre Defence Committee, Arrernte women disclosed
more and more details. Press releases were regularly issued and
videos, pamphlets and broadsheets were distributed through various networks both in Australia and overseas. In this publicity some
details were given of the meaning of the site to Arrernte women: it
was made clear, for example, that the site was associated with the
'Two Women Dreaming' and with women's breasts. Arrernte
women later seemed to suggest that this exclusive site mattered not
only to them but to 'all women'. Speaking of the ceremonies associated with the site, Arrernte woman, Rosie Kunoth-Monks, said:
'They are a vital part of being a woman. Like you've got women's
liberation, for hundreds of years we've had ceremonies which control our conduct, how we behave and act and how we control our
sexual lives. They give spiritual and emotional health to Aboriginal
women'.[7]

There were indeed many groups that came under the influence
of Welatye-Therre. Offers of support and monetary donations were
received from various branches of Women's Action Against Global
Violence, the Feminist Antinuclear Group, various women's health
centres and refuges, the Feminist Bookshop Sydney, Women for
Life, and the Women's International League for Peace and Freedom.

Environmental groups, like Greenpeace and Friends of the Earth, also offered their support, while the London-based Aboriginal Support Group made clear that their concern for the Arrernte struggle was also an investment in a global environmental future: 'We have all come to admire and respect the deep feeling Aboriginal people hold for their land and feel that we in Europe and people all over the world have much to learn from you in caring for the earth'.[8]

These sympathisers, environmentalist and feminist alike, came to Welatye-Therre because what little they knew of the site resonated with their own political agendas. Here was a site which hinted at the role indigenous people might play in an alternate environmental future; here was a site which spoke of an alternate structure of gender relations to a feminism now sensitised to difference but still drawn by the idea of universal solidarity. What these sympathisers did not know about the site, what remained unspoken, provided the space into which their imaginative hopes for an alternate world could flow. One way to read such a convergence would be in terms of a non-Aboriginal appropriation of an Aboriginal cause. But does that word 'appropriation', with all of its predatory overtones, suitably explain these sorts of affiliations?[9] We have already noted how Uluru is a site which, despite the efforts to reinstate some level of Aboriginal exclusivity, is opened up by the force of the uncontainable 'love' of the many others who visit it, are touched by it, or take it up into their own idiosyncratic geographies of significance. Like Uluru, the modern, public articulation of the specific and exclusive (secret) significance of Welatye-Therre could not be disentangled from the amplifications produced by the sympathies which attached themselves to the site and to the Arrernte cause. So a sacred site retains its socialising force but it is now a force which is uncontrollable in the sense that anyone can attach themselves to it. Socialisation now produces incoherence; an exclusive place is also, in its modern context, a 'promiscuous' place.

We might read this process of the sacred spiralling out of the confines of its localised geography under the force of sympathy as a positive thing: providing the basis for new affiliations which work to secure the site's significance and its ultimate protection. But when a second proposal was mooted for a flood mitigation dam and yet more 'Two Sister Dreaming' sites were placed under threat, the Arrernte women took a far more cautious approach to disclosing the content of the threatened sites. As one Arrernte women explained to Justice Hal Wooton, who presided over the inquiry into the Aboriginal significance of land which would be affected by the proposed dam:

> Only Traditional owners used to hear these stories that their grandparents told them. Now they are going to hear this story all over the place. This dam has made the story really come out into the open; the story that used to be really secret. Now other tribes are going to hear about it . . . now everybody is going to learn, and the white people as well are going to learn about it. The country story that used to be hidden. It was like that for Welatye Atherra . . . Now they know about that place all over the world, about the Dreaming as well . . . We are giving away all our secrets now, and it will be heard all over the world, if there is a protest against building the dam. We'll have to give away our secrets again.[10]

Disclosure, then, can bring gains in the form of new affiliations which work to intensify and enlarge the significance of a site. But it also brings some losses: a loss of exclusivity and a loss of control over the socialising force of the sacred. This Arrernte women expresses her own worries that the entry of their secrets into the public domain means that now too many people know about Arrernte business. What was once (exclusively) theirs is now also potentially anybody's. And just as it is not possible to know what is in the minds of those who are touched by a place like Uluru, so it is uncertain whether the new affiliations which are produced by disclosure are points of consensual sharing or points of predatory appropriation.

The Welatye-Therre case demonstrates the advantages and the hazards of sympathetic affiliations with the Aboriginal sacred. Let us now return to the other kind of affiliation we had noted earlier, one which is underwritten with scepticism. The 1994 claim by Ngarrindjeri women, that a secret women's site would be damaged by the construction of a bridge across the River Murray to link the mainland with Hindmarsh Island, drew exactly this kind of affiliation. In fact, the Ngarrindjeri claim had initially been recognised as believable enough by the then Federal Labor Minister for Aboriginal and Torres Strait Islander Affairs, Robert Tickner. On the advice of a report prepared by Professor Cheryl Saunders, he exercised his powers under the Aboriginal and Torres Strait Islander Protection Act (1984) and halted the construction of the bridge for a period of twenty-five years. For the South Australian government, however, this Federal intervention in local affairs was nothing but bad news since it had already become inextricably involved in this private–public development venture. Tickner's decision met with legal challenges from the developers, Tom and Wendy Chapman. Then in mid-1995 a group of Ngarrindjeri women publicly disputed the existence on Hindmarsh Island of secret sacred women's business. Soon afterwards a Ngarrindjeri man, Doug Milera, who had originally supported the claim, publicly admitted that the business the claim was based upon was, to use a word that had begun to circulate through the case, a 'fabrication'.[11] Later on, he confused the issue still further by recanting, as if the admission he had just made was a fabrication of a fabrication. In response to these various challenges and revelations the State government of South Australia appointed a Royal Commissioner to inquire into the Hindmarsh Bridge affair. The terms of reference for the Commission were like no other legal inquiry thus far into Aboriginal claims over land. The Hindmarsh Island Bridge Royal Commission (1995) was directed to investigate whether the claims by Ngarrindjeri women actually *were* a 'fabrication' and, if so, what was its 'extent' and 'purpose'.[12] It was an inquiry which, for sympathisers and sceptics alike, came to be emblematic of the nation's contemporary condition. For some, to disbelieve Aboriginal claims about Hindmarsh Island amounted to threatening 'the interests of a nation committed to reconciliation'.[13] For others, Hindmarsh Island became a testing ground for their suspicions that Aboriginal claims for sacredness were not only proliferating, but also making illegitimate (because they seem to be unverifiable) claims upon the nation. The right-wing sociologist John Carroll, from La Trobe University, took Hindmarsh Island as symptomatic of a change in the minds of Australian voters that saw the end of the Keating Labor government in March 1996 and the election of the Howard conservative coalition: 'Central to the March 2 revolt was a sense of betrayal by the elites . . . What was seen as indulging a series of minority interests, selected according to politically correct criteria—highlighted in the Hindmarsh Island fiasco—brought outrage because of what it indicated, the abandoning of middle Australia'.[14] Hindmarsh Island could hardly be more central to the nation's fortunes here, imagined as a luxury which was 'indulged' at the apparent expense of a majority ('middle Australia') which, in turn, is imagined as marginal and embattled.

The strangeness of this perspective lies in the way it takes the 'majority' as restrained, even disabled, in relation to minority indulgences (associated with 'elites'). Indeed, Carroll's remarks speak directly to the dispossession 'middle Australia' feels it has been dealt out by a nation which has seemed to give itself over so completely to 'indulged' minority groups such as Aboriginal people! We have already spoken about this uncanny view of modern, 'mainstream' Australia. But let us note how it came to be directly articulated in the Hindmarsh Island dispute through the fortunes of the developers themselves, Wendy and Tom Chapman, who had been virtually bankrupted by the delays to the proposed bridge. When Federal Court Judge Maurice O'Loughlin found in favour of the Chapmans and overturned the Federal government's ban on the bridge, he none the less added this less than flattering footnote: 'I am compelled to say that the litigation was unnecessarily prolonged as a result of their [that is, the Chapmans'] fixation that they have been the victims of a conspiracy to ignore their rights'.[15] In the wake of the judge's decision, Wendy Chapman is quoted as demanding: 'Give us back our possessions, give us back control of our destiny and allow us to get on with the development'.[16] This couple, then, become emblematic of a new social category: 'dispossessed middle Australians'. More to the point, they articulate their location in the 'mainstream' by invoking the imagery (dispossession, victimisation, rights, a 'fixated' single interest, 'prolonged' legal wranglings, self-determination) of the very same 'indulged' minority group they have been opposing: Aboriginal people.

At the centre of the Hindmarsh Island inquiry was the secret sacred women's business. Ngarrindjeri women revealed aspects of the secret business to Robert Tickner's investigator and then to the 'feminist anthropologist' appointed by the Aboriginal Legal Rights Movement to assist the women in preparing their case, Deane Fergie. But they also placed stipulations on the access the Minister and other government representatives could have to their secret information. The initial report to the Minister had two sealed envelopes appended which were marked 'To be read by women only'. Those sealed envelopes became suddenly notorious when, under circumstances which could only be described as obscure— and yes, politics has its obscurities, too—they unexpectedly came into the hands of the then Liberal shadow Minister for the Environment, Ian McLachlan. We call these circumstances 'obscure' rather than, say, 'accidental' because these envelopes were in a package that was, in fact, addressed to a senior Labor adviser to Tickner, Sean McLaughlin: someone from the other major political party whose name nevertheless bears an uncanny resemblance to the Liberal shadow minister's (but on the other hand, Hindmarsh Island lies in what was Ian McLachlan's electorate). This mix-up was exploited by Ian McLachlan's staffers who opened the package and photocopied the contents, including the sealed envelopes addressed only to women. Such a flagrant breach of confidentiality produced a scandal in which Ngarrindjeri women publicly grieved and successfully called for McLachlan's resignation. We see again, of course, that the Aboriginal sacred can reach into the political centre of the nation with devastating effects. Indeed, what is so fascinating about this scandal is that the envelopes themselves came to embody the sacredness attributed to Hindmarsh Island. By opening the envelopes, this Liberal politician was seen to have violated the exclusivity of the women's business of Hindmarsh Island, even though he was nowhere near the site itself.[17] We can pause here to wonder once more about the ability of a sacred site to travel under modern circumstances—in this particular case, channelled through (amongst other things) the unpredictable pathways of the Australian postal service. It is not just that there is no telling how and where one's sacred secrets may be received; it is also that there is no telling what form those sacred secrets might take. A site can even become a (purloined) letter.

The issue of secrecy also became central to the way in which the Commission conducted its own business of investigating 'fabrication'. In this context secrecy took on different and much more directed forms. Ngarrindjeri women who opposed the bridge began to give it a sometimes quite literal embodiment by boycotting the Commission hearings and by tying gags over their mouths in their street protests. Along with the sealed envelopes (where to look at their contents is to violate the sacred), these expressions of secrecy would seem to take us back to the structure of the differend which we discussed in Chapter 1. There we talked about the way in which Aboriginal people can be coded as 'mute' in the context of a court which requires them to talk but never understands what they say. The Hindmarsh Island Royal Commission does get close to this structure in the sense that these Aboriginal women's refusal to speak does indeed seem to produce a certain amount of incommensurability here with non-Aboriginal people. This chosen 'muteness' is certainly built around the presence of secrecy. But it is the very presence of secrecy which comes to unsettle the binary that the differend would otherwise leave intact. In the Hindmarsh Island case, secrecy was never a passive thing. It was never just, to recall Tom Griffiths' phrase, a 'dumb relic'. Its 'muteness' was always articulated and activated (the contents of a sealed envelope, a boycott, a gagged mouth), flowing through one public domain or another: if not the law courts, then a minister's office and its photocopying machine or a select street location or a media industry which is always so willing to listen and report. Indeed, the apparently promiscuous nature of secrecy in this affair—that it could flow into so many other places—was a matter of grave concern for the Royal Commission, which had already been worrying over the question of what it could or could not require to be 'divulged' about the women's sacred secret business.

The Commission had to operate in line with section 35 of the Aboriginal Heritage Act 1988 (SA), which outlawed the unauthorised divulgence of information relating to Aboriginal tradition. So the court was obliged to produce itself as a closed, restricted space, carefully abiding by the protocols attached to Aboriginal secrecy: not calling for the sealed envelopes to be submitted, not issuing subpoenas to the boycotting women, and so on. But at the same time it was acutely aware of information about the women's business being disclosed elsewhere, in other adjacent public forums. On 4 September 1995 the Commissioner ruled 'that the Commission may hear evidence of matters already widely published or generally available to the public in the Press, on radio or television, in books, reports or displays, or Court transcripts and exhibits'.[18] So the Commission recognised the need to restrict itself in order to preserve Aboriginal secrecy, even as it registered (enviously?) the fact that secrets were already being compromised in other public domains—to which the Commission felt it should have access. One lawyer, Michael Abbott, QC, complained to the Commissioner that Aboriginal women who could not be called upon to speak in the courts were nevertheless giving media interviews: 'They should not be allowed to disclose to (television personality) Ray Martin but not to you . . . They cannot have it both ways'.[19] We have thus come to an uncanny situation as far as secrecy is concerned. How can it be 'mute' in the courts if it is so continually compromised, so 'promiscuous', elsewhere? Should the courts, in order to preserve the 'muteness' of Aboriginal secrets, seal themselves off from this 'elsewhere' or entangle themselves in it? Is secrecy instrumental in the restriction of sacredness (within the law courts, for example), or does it actually assist in its amplification through entanglements that it inevitably gives rise to? How did the law courts come to give themselves over so completely (but not completely enough to prevent entanglements elsewhere) to this thing called 'Aboriginal secrecy'? Who is producing who in this postcolonial arrangement? Let us close this paragraph with the Royal Commission's observation about the role of anthropologist Deane Fergie, who herself felt bound to the confidentiality of secrecy in the frame of the court: 'she claimed', the Commissioner writes, 'that because of that undertaking she had no right to divulge information, *even if it was already publicly known*'.[20] How uncanny is this strange remark? It tells us that something (like the sealed envelopes) can continue to be unfamiliar, even when some of us might be already familiar with it!

And this can only happen when, notwithstanding one's commitment not to disclose, secrecy and publicity ceaselessly solicit one another, as they do in the making of the modern sacred.

What about the role of scepticism in the Hindmarsh Island affair? Amongst other things, this affair demonstrated that scepticism is not the sole privilege of non-Aboriginal people. The most unsettling feature of this case was that a group of other Ngarrindjeri women (and men) came out in opposition to the claims for Aboriginal sacredness. We can remember Durkheim's point about the ability of sacredness to cohere a social group, but here the issue of sacredness produced a profound internal division, fracturing rather than stabilising a community. Indeed, a whole number of communities were fractured by this case: the political community, the legal profession, the discipline of anthropology, the media, and so on. Ngarrindjeri women themselves split into two opposing groups: those who supported the claims for sacredness, the 'proponents', and those who did not believe those claims, the so-called 'dissidents'. In a book which was written in support of (and in tribute to) the dissident women, television journalist Chris Kenny outlines the divisions between the women in some detail. Kenny's project involves securing the fact that Aboriginal claims for sacredness were 'fabricated' by the 'proponents'. The scepticism of the 'dissident' women comes to provide the compelling evidence for his own latent logic of disbelief—as if Aboriginal people and non-Aboriginal people now have scepticism in common. In the process of providing evidence for fabrication, however, another narrative emerges. Kenny presents an account of a crucial meeting held between the women in April 1995 to discuss the secret sacred claims. This account turns on an exchange between one of the proponent women, Doreen Kartinyeri, and one of the dissident women, Dorothy Wilson, shortly after the latter had met with Liberal MHR Ian McLachlan. As part of this exchange, Dorothy Wilson complained that the content of the secret envelopes was familiar to others, but not to her: 'How come we've got white women who know what is in the secret envelopes . . . but none of us black women?'[21] This and other similar statements by Wilson focus not on the issue of 'fabrication', but the issue of exclusion: exclusion from the knowledges that sacred secrets might bring. In this respect, there is a sense that other women are privileged here, but the dissident women are not. Let us put this another way: some women are seen here to be in possession of sacred secrets, whereas others are seen to be dispossessed of these things. One of the questions which accompanied this splitting was, which group is then in the minority? These dispossessed, dissenting Aboriginal women had worked hard to dissociate themselves from a minority status: 'Most of them hated the term "dissident women" ', Kenny tells us, 'because they felt it made them sound like the minority—the breakaways. They have always maintained that they were standing up for mainstream Ngarrindjeri people and their beliefs'.[22] Can a 'dissident' minority ever represent the 'mainstream'? A Liberal Party employee, Sue Lawrie, went on to give this characterisation of the 'dissident' women's predicament: 'if Aboriginal women are the least empowered group in Australian society, how less empowered are the women who disagree with the power group within that group'?[23] For Lawrie, then, the minority status of these women is doubly secured: dispossessed (of secrecy) and disempowered together. Austin Gough drew upon his prefeminist (and colonial) sensibilities to defend these Aboriginal women as 'shy and diffident', thus giving these uncanny characteristics an extra twist by allowing the women to be seen as diffident and dissident at the same time![24]

Adelaide lawyer, Greg Mead, viewed the status of these women in a quite different way, however. Far from being 'mute' through their disempowerment, these women were, in fact, fully entangled in the kinds of powerful alliances that scepticism can produce:

> It might be said that they were not disempowered for long. Mr McLachlan, a senior member of the Liberal Party, had taken up their cause in Federal Parliament in November 1994 and again in March 1995. With the help of Mr McLachlan and Ms Lawrie this less empowered group were soon commanding substantial favourable media attention.[25]

When the Royal Commission found in favour of 'fabrication' just before Christmas in 1995, the dissident women became emblematic of a kind of 'commonsensical' mainstream Australian position on sacredness. The media was quick to relish the Commissioner's findings ('Lies, lies, lies'), feting the dissident women as embattled heroes who had, in Kenny's words, 'done . . . their country a great service'.²⁶ These so-called 'dissident' women thus came to stand for the nation itself, serving the interests of 'all of us'. Another dissident woman, Dulcie Wilson—in one of a number of public statements this group had made about the Hindmarsh Island affair—articulated this desire to align herself with the rest of the nation: 'I personally believe that the greatest injustice to Aborigines in this country was the labelling of them as *different*'.²⁷ So in relation to the interests of the nation, these women are claimed as 'dissident', even 'diffident', but not 'different'. It is this affiliation between a minority group and the national interest which makes these women both idiosyncratic and emblematic. They can be claimed by the nation (by the media, by politicians and so on) because they seem to have acted out a mutual scepticism towards the sacred. These women, far from being 'mute' or 'diffident', come to provide the Aboriginal voice mainstream Australia had been waiting to hear. There was no more uncanny an image of all this than the various front-page newspaper photographs of these dissident-yet-mainstream women taking tea together around a kitchen table in celebration of the fact that Hindmarsh Island was *not* a sacred site!

Reflecting the kind of split in allegiance that Hindmarsh Island had produced, Chris Kenny's book in defence of the 'dissident' women was countered by another book by lawyer, Greg Mead, which offered a completely opposite view of events: *A Royal Omission* (1995). In a very precise sense, these two books present narratives about the Hindmarsh Island affair which are incommensurable with each other but which each came to be broadly accepted. While Kenny unleashes scepticism over the possibility of sacred secrets, Mead respects Aboriginal people's right to secrecy and to their distinctive beliefs. His own scepticism turns instead upon the 'dissident' women's claims that there had indeed been a 'fabrication', a position that Kenny simply does not, and cannot, entertain. One reason why these two books are incommensurable with each other is that they divide scepticism and belief along party political lines.

Mead's scepticism, for example, forms around the affiliations established between the 'dissident' women, Liberal Party representatives and other right-wing sympathisers (such as Christopher Pearson, editor of the *Adelaide Review* and one of Prime Minister John Howard's speech-writers; or the Institute for Public Affairs). Chris Kenny, on the other hand, has the opposite axe to grind. He argues that the proponent women were activated through alliances with trade unions, radical feminist anthropologists, environmentalists and Labor politicians. In particular, he targets Robert Tickner, the then Labor Minister for Aboriginal and Torres Strait Islander Affairs, as a man who believed in Aboriginal secrets far too readily. These two books thus articulate a structure of affiliation which has been an all too apparent aspect of Aboriginal claims about sacred secrets: that the Right is sceptical ('rational', 'commonsensical', masculine), while the Left is gullible ('indulgent', feminine, too accommodating). This is a structure which allowed Liberal shadow minister Alexander Downer to comment on Labor's involvement in the Hindmarsh Island affair, in a speech calling for Tickner's resignation: 'What you people do the whole time is try to play the Aboriginal part—you like to play the black part'.[28] In the midst of claiming the 'dissident' women for the 'mainstream' nation, those who are actually mandated to represent the nation are coded as a minority group: 'Aboriginal'. This may be the only kind of difference remaining in a political field where the two parties have increasingly come to resemble each other: whether a politician supports the Aboriginal sacred with belief, or nullifies it with scepticism.

But does scepticism really nullify the Aboriginal sacred? Perhaps we should turn to Chris Kenny's account of how one of the 'dissident' women comes finally to reflect upon the way the Hindmarsh Island affair had changed her life. Speaking about Dorothy Wilson, Kenny writes: 'She still couldn't care less about the bridge, *but the island has assumed an importance in her life that she never thought possible*'.[29] While noting that the 'island never meant anything to us before', Wilson goes on to conclude: 'That place will always draw me now—I'll go there—it's become such a big part of my life'.[30] Kenny's scepticism, with all its powerful affiliations, thus talks up the significance of Hindmarsh Island *even as it tries to talk it down*. His book ends with the hope that he might be able to 'forget about Hindmarsh Island and get on with my life'.[31] But, in fact, he produces Hindmarsh Island as a place which now simply cannot be forgotten, a place to which even 'dissident' disbelievers now find themselves drawn. Let us close this chapter by noting the uncanny consequence of this structure: that when scepticism turns to a place that 'never meant anything . . . before' and becomes utterly entangled with it, it transforms that place into nothing less than a 'site of significance' with such immense reach and such powers of affect that even the sceptics themselves succumb to it.

Conclusion

On *Wik*, Postcolonial
Democracy and Other Matters

OUR READINGS of the Aboriginal sacred in modern Australia have turned upon a recognition of its potential unboundedness, and the ways in which this unboundedness can effect—or affect—the nation's sense of itself. Indeed, a certain amount of unfamiliarity can arise when the sacred is so unbounded, where 'modern Australia' itself becomes an ambivalent thing, required ceaselessly to engage with structures it may have imagined as, at best, anachronistic. The nation becomes unfamiliar to itself precisely because of a postcolonial condition in which an indigenous population is increasingly able not just to 'write back' but to produce a range of special effects which can be unsettling right across the board. To recall Julia Kristeva's comment, we can wonder whether to 'smile' or to 'worry' in response to these unsettlements: should we celebrate them or see them as a cause for anxiety? All we can really say about this is that it depends upon one's nostalgias (for example, for a secure connection between language and place, for 'tradition', for authority) and one's political and cultural affiliations (for example, with mining interests, with the 'guilt industry', with the 'rationality' of scepticism or the 'irrationality' of enthralment, with ways of writing history and reading culture, with ambivalence itself).

The Australian High Court decision providing for common law recognition of Aboriginal prior occupation of Australia and culminating in the first nationally conceived Native Title Act 1993 (the so-called *Mabo* decision) no doubt gave this process of unsettlement-in-the-midst-of-modernity a certain intensification. *Terra nullius*, the founding fantasy of modern Australian

135

nationhood, was rejected by this ruling and Aboriginal people were given the opportunity to make claims over a much wider range of lands than had previously been provided for under existing land rights legislation. The rejection of *terra nullius* was read by some as the moment when a great deal of Australia might become available for Aboriginal reclamation. In fact—and in keeping with previous land rights provisions—what can be claimed, and by which Aboriginal groups, is quite limited. Nevertheless, especially for those non-Aboriginal people who (even momentarily) may have entertained the possibility of losing their homes to Aboriginal claims to land, *Mabo* produced a great deal of 'worry' and very few 'smiles', at the very moment when Australia was talking openly about 'reconciliation'.

The *Wik* decision of 23 December 1996 came in the wake of *Mabo*, as a landmark ruling by the High Court which lent support to the national project of 'reconcilation' by advocating the 'co-existence' of Aboriginal and pastoralists' rights to leaseholds in northern Queensland. The Wik and Thayorre people responded to the spirit of this decision by saying that 'there were no losers'.[1] Yet this same decision was immediately received by other social groups (pastoralists, in particular) as a 'failure'. These people took 'co-existence' to signify nothing other than their own loss: as if it some-how reduced the 'properness' of their access to leasehold land. So 'co-existence', like 'reconciliation', immediately became irreconcil-able with itself. It immediately began to suggest imbalance, in-equality. The Prime Minister, John Howard, became entangled in this issue, noting in the first instance that the High Court's advocacy of 'co-existence' had meant that 'the pendulum had swung too far towards Aborigines and had to be reset'.[2] Pressured by pastoralists and National Party members, the coalition government began to talk of the 'blanket extingushment' of Aboriginal rights to leasehold land, reanimating the colonial fantasy of *terra nullius* that the earlier *Mabo* decision had overturned. But this colonial fantasy operated through the frame of a postcolonial racism whereby 'extinguishment' was required though only in the context of the (mis)recognition that Aboriginal people now have 'too much'. This (mis)recognition then enabled the most powerful social group in the country to represent themselves as an embattled minority. It is often pointed out that pastoralists constitute some of Australia's wealthiest people and corporations: Kerry Packer's Consolidated Pastoral Company, the federal president of the National Party (who is the country's second-largest private landholder), Janet Holmes à Court's Heytesbury Pastoral Company, and so on.[3] Nevertheless, the case that pastoralists presented against the *Wik* decision relied upon casting themselves not only as embattled, but utterly impotent. In a public letter to John Howard, the 'farmers of Australia' spoke plaintively of their case:

> But we may not be strong enough to survive this uncertainty over our lives, our ability to manage our farms and the right of our children to inherit them. We're worried sick about this Wik decision.
>
> After all, John, if you were farming on a pastoral lease would you invest every cent you could scrape together in buildings, fences, dams and trees, if a court could decide at any time that someone shared your land?[4]

The impotence mobilised by pastoralists, of course, relies here on reinventing themselves as 'farmers'—who, as freeholders, are actually untouched by the *Wik* decision but who can appear vulnerable all the same through their non-corporate (that is, family-based) identity. This helped to sentimentalise the pastoralists' case. But it was also an expansionist manoeuvre, for it positioned leasehold pastoralists as somehow lacking the security of tenure that 'farmers' enjoy even as they anticipated access to that security by claiming the identity of 'farmers' for themselves. One of the central debates following the *Wik* decision was about the possibility of leasehold pastoralists becoming freeholders, and thus themselves having more than their 'proper' share. So the pastoralists designate themselves as an embattled, impotent minority in order then to be able to claim rights they have never been able to claim before. Indeed—and this is the uncanny feature of this process—by imagining themselves as a minority, the pastoralists are then able to stride right into the centre of the national consciousness and demand its attention: 'And who will feed Australia then?' they wonder, apocalyptically fancying their *own* 'extinguishment'.[5] These manoeuvrings and imaginings produce a crisis for the kind of representative democracy that requires 'reconciliation' or 'co-existence' as the means by which 'all of us' may be governed equally. Dr Wendy Craik, the National Farmers Federation executive director, spoke for representative democracy when she reminded the Prime Minister that 'he has got to take everybody's interests into account' in relation to the *Wik* decision. But on the same day, the presidents of three conservative State parties issued quite the opposite directive to John Howard: 'We trust the Prime Minister *will . . . not fail Australia by trying to please all parties*, and allow a running sore to develop on the national fabric'.[6] So how can democracy in a postcolonial nation 'take everybody's interests into account' while at the same time be called upon not 'to please all parties'? No wonder political commentator, Shaun Carney, could see Prime Minister Howard as 'a man caught in a long, bad dream': 'Native title', he remarks, 'is the substance of the nightmare'.[7]

We have used the uncanny in this book to elaborate a modern Australian condition where what is 'ours' may also be 'theirs', and vice versa: where difference and 'reconciliation' co-exist uneasily. In an uncanny Australia, one's place is always already another's place and the issue of possession is never complete, never entirely settled. The conventional colonial distinctions between self and other, here and there, mine and yours, are now by no means totally determinable; a certain unboundedness occurs whereby the one inhabits the other at one point, disentangles itself at another, inhabits it again, and so on, in a relationship we have designated as soliciting. This is why, for example, boundaries designed to distinguish the one from the other are so hard to draw in modern Australia and, if they *are* drawn, they are immediately absorbed into a process of use (a politics) which can utterly transform the distinctions they had sought to make. We can think about this process as a way in which 'place', as a designation which implies boundedness or restriction, is always at the same time in a condition of unboundedness. So one can never be completely in possession of place: one is always (dis)possessed, in the sense that neither possession nor dispossession is a fully realisable category. In the same way, one's authority over a place always entails a certain 'arbitrariness'. We have produced a number of equations so far to articulate these conditions—tradition is (not) modern; a site is (not) the nation, and so on—and we see these equations as appropriate to a postcolonial context. Indeed, the aim of this book has been as follows: we want to contemplate the possibility of producing a postcolonial narrative which, rather than falling into a binary that either distinguishes 'us' from 'them' or brings us all together as the same, would instead think through the uncanny implications of being in place and 'out of place' at precisely the same time.

Of course, the politics of a postcolonial nation like Australia ceaselessly (mis)recognises this, moving back and forth between positions as if they are always disentangled: separation or incommensurability as distinct from 'reconciliation' or 'co-existence'; a 'divided nation' as opposed to 'one nation'. Each position seems somehow to involve a choice which then turns out to be compromised by the other from which it sought to distinguish itself. Take, for example, the term 'one nation', which has utterly inverted itself in the last decade. Under Paul Keating's Labor government, 'one nation' had stood for unity-through-difference, tolerantly bringing multicultural identities together under the one national umbrella. By the mid-1990s, however, 'one nation' was the name given by Pauline Hanson to a fledgling political party which could only conceive of the nation in terms of unity-through-sameness. But this very conception of unity-through-sameness produced an ongoing sequence of protests and disavowals right across the country. It was not only that the notion of 'one nation' was utterly transformed in the process; it came, finally (and once again), to signify exactly what it had been distinguished from: a 'divided nation'.

Does this mean that Australia ceaselessly (mis)recognises itself? The Australian Mining Industry Council—before it became the Minerals Council of Australia—provided one spectacular instance where (mis)recognition played itself out once more. During their 1993 campaign against the introduction of Native Title legislation, AMIC produced a number of full-page advertisements in the major daily newspapers. One of these advertisements featured a land-use map of Australia with special attention drawn to land already under

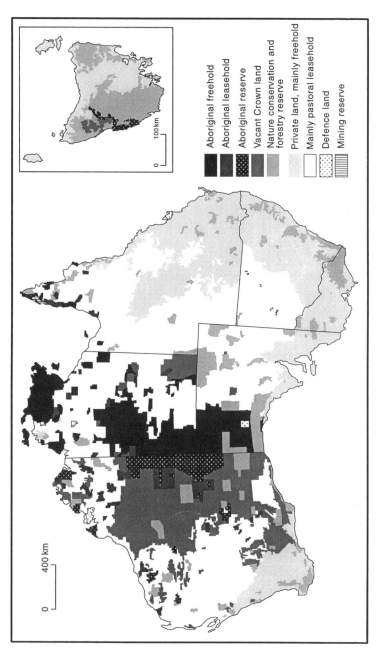

Figure 2 This map of contemporary land use in Australia—which showed among other things lands claimed, or available to be claimed, by Aboriginal people—became the basis for the Australian Mining Industry Council's anxious advertisement campaign against native title: 'Does it look', they asked, 'anything like the one we studied at school?' (Adapted from Australian Survey and Land Information Group, *Public Land, Aboriginal and Torres Strait Islander Land*, edition 19, 1993).

Aboriginal control (Figure 2). AMIC adjusted this map by marking in nine additional regions around the nation which were subject to claims under the Native Title provisions. The text of their advertisement (which the Minerals Council asked us not to reproduce in full, given their current change in direction) urged Australians to look again at the place in which we live: 'Take a good look at this map. Does it look anything like the one we studied at school?'[8] The answer, of course, was supposed to be 'No'. Non-Aboriginal Australians, aligned to AMIC under the collective pronoun 'we', were supposed to see this as an unfamiliar rendering of their nation: it is not the place they have been used to. It is not 'like the one we studied at school': it is not the homely, settled Australia that colonisation was supposed to have produced. Much of the anxiety here lay in the fact that the boundaries represented on this map seemed likely to change: to become unsettled, unpredictable. In fact, the map, as AMIC as re-presented it in their advertisement, worked by laying an anticipated future over the top of Australia as it presently is to suggest the impossibility of 'co-existence' between these two moments. AMIC thus return in their advertisement to the views they expressed in *Shrinking Australia* two years earlier: that Aboriginal ownership presupposes an exclusivity ('single interest') that renders it incommensurable with other kinds of land uses. Those pre-Oedipal days when one could speak without irony of 'we'—'all of us', as Australians together, without difference—seemed for AMIC at this juncture to be well and truly over.

The 1993 AMIC advertisement presented a particular version of postcolonial racism, one which we have seen before in this book and which is often expressed in contemporary Australia, when they stated: 'Right now, Aboriginal people constitute 1.5% of Australia's population. And yet they already have title to, or reserves for 14% of Australia's land area'.[9] We have already noted this tendency to imagine Aboriginal people as 'expansionist', and our brief discussion of the *Wik* case above was aimed to temper this (mis)recognition by reminding readers that others can secure their own expansions by appealing to this image. But what are the political implications of these anxious responses which imply that Aboriginal people, far from being 'out of place' in the nation, now have too many places altogether? For those of us who are familiar with the 'Australian tradition' of liberal history ('the one we studied at school . . .'), something quite uncanny may have occurred. Liberal history, with its egalitarian, representative, democratic base, had often signalled the injustice of an Australia in which a small percentage of people—the wealthy—owned (and still own) a disproportionately large percentage of the country. Such a structure was rightly seen as undemocratic and anti-egalitarian. Yet those people who support Aboriginal land claims can find themselves facing a mirror image of this structure in postcolonial Australia. At what point does the production of equity—in this case, the sympathetic underwriting of Aboriginal claims for land they have lost—seem to become disproportionate to itself? When it is perceived in this way, an uncanny experience can follow because such a mutation implies that the compensatory mechanisms of the democratic 'tradition', those procedures which worked towards equity, are internally compromised.

The logic of AMIC and others in their wake would have us believe that it is quite undemocratic for a small percentage of Aboriginal people to own so much of Australia. But what exactly are the limits of representative democracy in such postcolonial redistributions of space? How much land surface can a minority group reasonably occupy before the arrangement can be considered as undemocratic (in terms of equity for 'all of us')? How much Aboriginal reterritorialisation can occur before the appeasement of 'guilt' transforms itself into the formation of resentment? When does compensation (for loss) get (mis)recognised as expansionism (gaining too much)? At what moment in this entanglement does postcolonial racism flourish? When do 'smiles' become 'worries'? It is here, again, that the arbitrariness of the sign makes its presence felt, since there is never any settled relationship in a postcolonial nation between what is democratic and the amount of space one might legitimately occupy. Of course, one uncanny effect of all this is the unsettlement of one's assumptions about who exactly can claim a 'proper' minority status—and we have seen pastoralists, as well as mining companies and developers and 'mainstream' Australia, do just this for themselves. When even the richest social groups in Australia can lay claim to 'minority' identities, what happens to redistributive, representational democracy in this country?

Under the instability of minoritarian arrangements in postcolonial Australia, the democratic 'tradition' is rendered incommensurable with itself even as it continues to remain 'in place' as traditions usually do. To point to such instabilities is not to suggest that familiar political projects should be abandoned. Our book has been neither pessimistic nor sceptical about the redistributive powers of postcoloniality; indeed, as far as scepticism is concerned, we have been at pains to show that even when something is being talked down, it is always at the same time activated and given new potential. Rather, we are simply suggesting that the kind of postcolonial narrative we have been trying to shape through these pages might nevertheless need to build an uncanny experience of democracy into its structure.

Notes

Introduction

[1] 'Scientist appeals for fair Deal', *Age*, 21 October 1996, p. 1.

1 The Modern Sacred

[1] R. Williams, 'Dominant, residual, and emergent', *Marxism and Literature*, pp. 121–7.

[2] See R. Brunton, *Blocking Business: An Anthropological Assessment of the Hindmarsh Island Dispute*.

[3] H. Morgan, 'The dire implications of Coronation Hill', pp. 36–7.

[4] Morgan, 'The dire implications', p. 35.

[5] E. Durkheim, *The Elementary Forms of the Religious Life*, p. 1; our italics.

[6] Ibid., p. 47; Durkheim's italics. For a discussion of Australia as a 'moral community' after *Mabo* (although it makes no mention of Durkheim) see T. Rowse, 'Mabo and Moral Anxiety'. Rowse is pessimistic about his topic: 'it is no easy matter to imagine Australia to be a "moral community"' (p. 230), that is, a coherent social group. This is because the 'moral traditions of Aborigines, the moral traditions of non-Aborigines, and the points of congruence and difference between them are all matters of dispute' (p. 249).

[7] Durkheim, *The Elementary Forms*, p. 8.

[8] Ibid., p. 6; our italics.

[9] Ibid.

[10] Ibid., p. 6n.

[11] Ibid., p. v.

[12] Ibid., p. 1.

[13] Ibid., pp. 440–1.

[14] Ibid., p. 422.

[15] M. Richardson, *Georges Bataille*, p. 74; our italics.

[16] D. Hollier, ed., *The College of Sociology (1937–39)*, p. xvi.

[17] Hollier, *The College of Sociology*, pp. xxiv and xi–xii.

[18] M. Leiris, 'The sacred in everyday life', p. 31; Leiris' italics.

[19] Hollier, *The College of Sociology*, p. xxiv.

[20] D. Tacey, *Edge of the Sacred: Transformation in Australia*, pp. 6 and 122.

[21] Ibid., pp. 50 and 187.

[22] Ibid., p. 193.

[23] Ibid., p. 194.

[24] Ibid., pp. 179 and 180.

[25] Ibid., p. 188.

[26] In the 1992 *Mabo* decision the High Court of Australia found in favour of Eddie Mabo's claim that the 1879 annexation of the Torres Strait was unlawful and in no way extinguished his customary ownership. This decision consolidated into the Native Title Act (1993).

[27] Tacey, *Edge of the Sacred*, p. 138.

[28] Ibid., p. 206.

[29] Durkheim, *The Elementary Forms*, p. 8.

[30] Tacey, *Edge of the Sacred*, p. 160.

[31] Ibid., p. 148.

[32] 'Racism row distracts Liberals', *Age*, 28 February 1996.

[33] Ibid.

[34] 'Race to the polls raises questions of Katter's "racist" remarks', *Age*, 28 February 1996.

[35] 'The New Racists are in charge', *Herald Sun*, 29 February 1996.

[36] For an account which prefers 'shame' to 'guilt', see 'Shame of the nation', *Age*, 28 August 1995.

[37] J-F. Lyotard, *The Differend: Phrases in Dispute*, p. xi.

[38] 'The effect on the Jawoyn outweighs economic benefit', *Australian Financial Review*, 19 June 1991, p. 8. Edited text of Prime Minister Bob Hawke's statement on Coronation Hill.

[39] Williams, 'Dominant, residual, and emergent', p. 122.

[40] B. Readings, *Introducing Lyotard: Art and Politics*, p. 118.

[41] J. Derrida, 'Différance', *Margins of Philosophy*, p. 16n.

2 The Postcolonial Uncanny

[1] S. Freud, 'The "Uncanny"', in A. Dickson (ed.), *The Pelican Freud Library: Art and Literature*, pp. 342–7.

[2] J. Kristeva, *Strangers to Ourselves*, pp. 171–3.

[3] Ibid., p. 182.

[4] Freud, 'The "Uncanny"', p. 346.

[5] Ibid., p. 347.

[6] Kristeva, *Strangers to Ourselves*, p. 191.

[7] R. Gibson, *South of the West: Postcolonialism and the Narrative Construction of Australia*, p. x.

[8] Ibid., p. xii.

[9] Ibid., p. 72.

[10] Ibid., p. 18.

[11] Ibid., pp. 91–2.

[12] Kristeva, *Strangers to Ourselves*, p. 191.

[13] R. Campbell Praed, 'The Bunyip', p. 108.

[14] Ibid., p. 103.

[15] Ibid., p. 105.

[16] Ibid., p. 106.

[17] P. Mumbulla, 'The Bunyip', p. 250.

[18] Ibid., p. 251.

[19] Ibid., p. 250.

[20] Ibid., p. 251.

[21] In Peter Read's *Returning to Nothing: The Meaning of Lost Places*, non-Aboriginal attachments to place are explored through the experience of losing your place—to a cyclone, for instance, in the case of Darwin residents. Loss actually intensifies the attachment to place, according to this book.

3 The Sacred (in the) Nation

[1] K. Maddock, 'Metamorphosing the sacred in Australia', p. 213.

[2] Ibid., p. 215.

[3] Ibid., pp. 216–17.

[4] Maddock notes that Ronald Berndt had a different view of sacredness, focusing on its 'derivation', rather than on the practices of exclusion which surrounded it: ibid., p. 217.

[5] Ibid., p. 226.

[6] K. Maddock, *Your Land is Our Land: Aboriginal Land Rights*, p. 131.

[7] Ibid., p. 133.

[8] Ibid., p. 148.

[9] Ibid.

[10] Ibid., p. 150.

[11] Ibid., p. 151.

[12] Ibid.

[13] R. Kelly, 'Why we bother', pp. 99–100.

[14] Ibid., p. 100.

[15] Ibid.

[16] Ibid., p. 98.

[17] S. Muecke, *Textual Spaces: Aboriginality and Cultural Studies*, p. 17.

[18] Ibid., p. 9.

[19] Ibid.

[20] Ibid.

[21] Ibid., p. 137.

[22] Australian Mining Industry Council, *Shrinking Australia: Australia's Economic Future: Access to Land*, pp. 1, 3.

[23] AMIC supports government policies which promote 'multiple land use' as opposed to 'single interest' land use. Ibid., p. 3.

[24] We acknowledge that the Minerals Council of Australia has changed direction in the way it manages issues affecting the mining industry and may no longer hold the views expressed in the 1990 *Shrinking Australia* document.

[25] 'If we get MABO wrong. We'll all lose, again', p. 9.

[26] Anon., 'Sorting out the mess that's Territory mining', *Australia's Mining Monthly*, 1992, p. 39.

[27] C. Anderson, 'Need for more micro-economic reform', p. 7.

[28] In line with the modern unsettlement of the bond between language and place, we need not go along with AMIC's tendency to imagine that its own interests exactly

resemble the interests of the nation. For an account which wonders about just how few Australians really do subscribe to AMIC's point of view, see 'Mabo scaremongers distort truth with statistics', p. 13.

29 It is not just that someone like Western Mining's Hugh Morgan can appeal to John Locke on the question of tolerance; more obscure, aberrant historical figures are invoked, too, as in an article by Mark Raynor, Group Executive of CRA Ltd, which notes that anti-mining lobbies 'are, whether they know it or not, heeding the advice of the 17th Century French ecclesiastic and politician Cardinal de Retz who held that, "the best way to compel weak-minded people to adopt our opinion, is to terrify them from all others, by magnifying their danger"': M. Raynor, 'Uncertainty: risks in decision making', p. 25. Who else would dream of taking Cardinal de Retz as a point of origin for modern-day environmental anxieties!

30 L. McIntosh 'Land access and the shrinking world of mining', p. 7.

31 Ibid., p. 9.

32 Ibid., p. 10.

33 Ibid., p. 11.

34 Raynor, 'Uncertainty', p. 25.

35 S. L. Davis and J. R. V. Prescott, *Aboriginal Frontiers and Boundaries in Australia*, p. xii.

36 Ibid., p. xiii.

37 Ibid., p. 25.

38 Ibid., p. 18.

39 Ibid., p. 24.

40 This map is referred to by Davis et al. as a 'national snapshot in time' of the spatial organisation of 'Aboriginal groups which have retained strong tradition-based links to territory': S. L. Davis, Resource Managers Pty Ltd and the Australian Mining Industry Council, *Australia's Extant and Imputed Traditional Aboriginal Territories*, map notes.

41 Davis and Prescott, *Aboriginal Frontiers and Boundaries*, p. xii.

42 Ibid., pp. 146–7, for example.

43 A. Lattas, 'Aborigines and contemporary Australian nationalism: primordiality and the cultural politics of otherness', pp. 50–69; N. Thomas, *Colonialism's Culture: Anthropology, Travel and Government*.

44 T. Grey, *Jabiluka: The Battle to Mine Australia's Uranium*, p. 118.

45 Ibid., p. 213.

46 Ibid., p. 233.

47 Ibid., p. 193.

48 In fact, the delays caused by negotiations with the NLC resulted in Pancon diversifying its operations, exploring mining possibilities in Canada, and seeking out French investors: ibid., pp. 224–5.

49 Ibid., p. 248.

50 Ibid., p. 228.

51 Ibid., p. 219.

52 Ibid., p. 229. Meaghan Morris notes that Mick Dundee offers a similar point of view: see 'Tooth and claw: tales of survival, and *Crocodile Dundee*', in *The Pirate's Fiancée: Feminism, Reading, Postmodernism*, pp. 241–69.

53 Ibid., p. 284.

54 'Rationality is fine, when it suits us', *Canberra Times*, 26 March 1995, p. 9; our italics.

4 Where is the Sacred?

1 W. Arndt, 'The Nargorkun-Narlinji cult', p. 299.

2 Ibid., p. 304.

3 Ibid., p. 299.

4 Ibid., p. 300.

5 Ibid.

6 Ibid., p. 319.

7 Ibid., p. 300.

8 F. Merlan, quoted in D. Cooper, *Report for the Registration of the Upper South Alligator Bula complex*, p. 17.

9 See, for example, K. Maddock, 'Yet another "sacred site": the Bula controversy', p. 133.

10 I. Keen and F. Merlan, *The Significance of the Conservation Zone to Aboriginal People*.

11 S. L. Davis and J. R. V. Prescott, *Aboriginal Frontiers and Boundaries*, p. 76.

12 Ibid.

13 Ibid., p. 79.

14 Ibid.

15 F. Merlan, 'The limits of cultural constructionism: the case of Coronation Hill', p. 341.

16 Keen and Merlan, *The Significance of the Conservation Zone to Aboriginal People*, p. 78, as cited in Merlan, 'The limits of cultural constructionism', p. 345.

17 Merlan, 'The limits of cultural constructionism', p. 349.

18 Ibid., p. 348.

19 R. Brunton, *The Significance of Shallow Traditions: The Resource Assessment Commission on Aboriginal Interests in Kakadu*, p. 1.

20 Hostages to a Bula legend', *Australian*, 2 May 1991, p. 11.

21 'Digging for an excuse', *Herald Sun*, 28 May 1991, p. 12.

22 Brunton, *The Significance of Shallow Traditions*, p. 3.

23 R. Brunton, 'Controversy in the Sickness Country: the battle over Coronation Hill', p. 18.

24 Ibid.

25 Ibid.

26 Ibid., p. 20.

27 K. Maddock, 'God, Caesar and Mammon at Coronation Hill', p. 306.

28 H. Morgan, 'The dire implications of Coronation Hill', p. 36.

29 'Coronation Hill test for sacred sites', *Australian*, 9 May 1991, p. 2.

30 '"Sickness Country" may become a national epidemic', *Weekend Australian*, 22–23 June 1991, p. 40.

31 'Kerin exalts Coronation Hill as "totem issue" for business', *Australian Financial Review*, 12 June 1991, p. 4.

32 E. Durkheim, *The Elementary Forms of the Religious Life*, pp. 124, 134.

33 'Not just a sacred site, also a political totem', *Age*, 20 June 1991, p. 13.

34 'Coronation Hill may be PM's answer to his son', *Age*, 18 June 1991, p. 15.

5 The Return of the Sacred

1 T. Griffiths, *Hunters and Collectors: The Antiquarian Imagination in Australia*, pp. 278–9.
2 W. Benjamin, 'Unpacking My Library', p. 69.
3 Griffiths, *Hunters and Collectors*, p. 42; our italics.
4 Ibid., p. 22.
5 C. Pardoe, 'Arches of Radii, corridors of power: reflections on current archaeological practice', p. 139.
6 'Mungo woman returns to her people', *Age*, 13 January 1992, p. 1.
7 'Mungo woman back to the dreamtime', *Age*, 18 January 1992, p. 14.
8 D. J. Mulvaney, 'Past regained, future lost: the Kow Swamp Pleistocene burials', pp. 12, 17, 21.
9 Ibid., p. 17.
10 Ibid., p. 20.
11 T. Murray, 'Aborigines, archaeology and Australian heritage', p. 726; our italics.
12 Ibid., p. 734.
13 Ibid., p. 727.
14 Ibid., p. 734.
15 Ibid., p. 733.
16 Ibid., p. 727.
17 Ibid., p. 731.
18 Ibid., p. 734.
19 Ibid., p. 734; our italics.
20 Pardoe, 'Arches of Radii', p. 140; Pardoe's italics.
21 C. Anderson, 'Aboriginal people and museums: restricting access to increase it', pp. 11–12.
22 C. Anderson, 'The economies of sacred art: The uses of a secret collection in the South Australian Museum', p. 101.
23 Ibid., p. 100.
24 Ibid., pp. 105–6.
25 Ibid., p. 106.
26 Here we are paraphrasing some choice remarks from Richard Dienst, *Still Life in Real Time: Theory After Television*, p. xii.
27 Anderson, 'Aboriginal people and museums', p. 12.
28 C. Anderson, 'Australian Aborigines and museums—A new relationship', pp. 173–4.
29 Anderson, 'The economics of sacred art', pp. 102, 104; Anderson, 'Australian Aborigines and museums', p. 177.
30 Anderson, 'Australian Aborigines and museums', p. 178.
31 C. Anderson in J. Roberts (dir.), *Sacred Journey*; our italics.

6 Authorising Sacredness

1 D. Jeater, 'Roast beef and reggae music: the passing of whiteness', p. 107.
2 P. Cochrane, 'Race memory', p. 8.
3 M. Taussig, *The Nervous System*, p. 124.
4 Ibid., p. 116.

5   S. Muecke, *Textual Spaces: Aboriginality and Cultural Studies*, pp. 65, 89–90.

6   Ibid., p. 116.

7   Ibid., p. 102.

8   Ibid., p. 116.

9   Ibid., p. 108.

10 Ibid., p. 103.

11 Ibid., p. 104.

12 Ibid.

13 Ibid., p. 109.

14 E. Durkheim, *The Elementary Forms of the Religious Life*, p. 55.

15 W. Benjamin, 'The Storyteller', p. 87; our italics.

16 'When bad omens come in boats', *Age*, 11 January 1997, Saturday Extra, p. 6.

17 See A. P. Elkin, *Aboriginal Men of High Degree*. For accounts of kadaitcha men, see also R. M. Berndt and C. H. Berndt, *The World of the First Australians*, pp. 324–5.

18 'Liberty taken with the legends', *Sunday Herald*, 5 August 1990.

19 S. Watson, *The Kadaitcha Sung*, p. 220.

20 Ibid., p. 182.

21 V. Johnson, 'Poetic justice', p. 34.

22 Durkheim, *Elementary Forms*, p. 55; our italics.

23 Watson, *The Kadaitcha Sung*, p. 215.

24 J. Marcus, 'The journey out to the Centre: the cultural appropriation of Ayers Rock', pp. 254–74.

25 B. Hill, *The Rock: Travelling to Uluru*, pp. 270–1; our italics.

26 Ibid., p. 1.

27 T. Rowse, 'Hosts and guests at Uluru', p. 257.

28 Cited in ibid., p. 257.

29 'Liberty taken with the legends'.

30 S. Watson, 'I say this to you', p. 591.

7 Promiscuous Sacredness

1   W. Arndt, 'The Nargorkun-Narlinji cult', p. 300.

2   See R. Brunton, *Blocking Business: An Anthropological Assessment of the Hindmarsh Island Dispute*.

3   C. Kenny, *'It Would Be Nice if There was Some Women's Business': The story behind the Hindmarsh Island affair*, p. 103. Kenny took the title for his exposé of the 'fabrication' of the Hindmarsh Island women's business from a statement reportedly made about the Hindmarsh Island claim by anthropologist Lindy Worrell, who was then 'working on women's sites' in northern South Australia (p. 71).

4   A. Gough, 'Hindmarsh Island and the politics of the future', p. 3.

5   Ibid., p. 4.

6   'Blacks fight plan to flood sacred site', *Age*, 22 April 1983, p. 1.

7   Rosie Kunoth-Monks, quoted in Welatye-Therre Defence Committee, *Voices from Mparntwe*, p. 1.

8   Aboriginal Support Group, London, quoted in *Welatye-Therre Defence Committee, Voices from Mparntwe*, p. 2.

[9] Meaghan Morris has suggested that appropriation does not need to be read simply as 'violence' or 'invasion'; it might also be seen as a point of 'negotiation' in the 'evolution of ... consensus'. See M. Morris, *The Pirate's Fiancée: Feminism, Reading, Postmodernism*, pp. 260 and 267.

[10] Justice H. Wootton, *Significant Aboriginal Sites in Areas of Proposed Junction Waterhole Dam, Alice Springs. Report to the Minister for Aboriginal Affairs*, p. 74.

[11] Chris Kenny quotes Milera as using the precise term 'fabricated' (Kenny, '*It Would be Nice . . .* , p. 181) but Greg Mead suggests that this word was used for the first time some six months earlier by the then Liberal shadow Environment Minister, Ian McLachlan, in an address to the House of Representatives in Canberra, and that the term began to circulate in the public domain subsequently. See Greg Mead, *A Royal Omission: A Critical Summary of the Evidence Given to the Hindmarsh Island Bridge Royal Commission with an Alternative Report*, p. 128.

[12] I. E. Stevens, *Report of the Hindmarsh Island Royal Commission*, p. 3.

[13] Editorial, *Australian*, 11 December 1995.

[14] J. Carroll, 'Howard's forgotten people', p. 32.

[15] Judge M. O'Loughlin, *Chapman and Others* v. *Tickner and Others*, p. 340.

[16] O'Loughlin, *Chapman and Others*, p. 133.

[17] For Chris Kenny, the violation of confidentiality appears to be a natural feature of a politician's life: before McLachlan 'was even told the box had arrived', Kenny writes, 'it had been opened, its contents photocopied and the originals sent on to Tickner. Ian McLachlan, a first class cricketer, viewed all that as fair play. 'Politicians deal in leaked documents as an everyday stock in trade. It was a windfall' (Kenny, '*It Would be Nice . . .*', p. 134). It seems odd to connect violation and fair play in the same breath; it is odder still to invoke cricket as the grounding metaphor for governmental disdain for other people's secrets.

[18] Stevens, *Report*, p. 14.

[19] 'Secrets to stay sealed', *Advertiser*, 2 November 1995, p. 2.

[20] Stevens, *Report*, p. 17; our italics.

[21] Kenny, '*It Would be Nice . . .*', p. 147.

[22] Ibid., p. 234.

[23] Cited in Mead, *A Royal Omission*, p. 173.

[24] Gough, 'Hindmarsh Island', p. 4.

[25] Mead, *A Royal Omission*, p. 173.

[26] 'Lies, lies, lies', *Advertiser*, 22 December 1995; Kenny, '*It Would be Nice . . .*', p. 9.

[27] D. Wilson, 'Telling the truth', p. 39; our italics.

[28] 'SA poised to probe bridge saga', *Advertiser*, 8 June 1995, p. 2.

[29] Kenny, '*It Would be Nice . . .*', p. 242; our italics.

[30] Cited in ibid.

[31] Ibid., p. 246.

Conclusion

[1] 'Ruling fails to end Title conflict', *Age*, 24 December 1996.

[2] 'Doing battle in a land long shared', *Age*, 9 June 1997.

3 'Who are the Wik winners?', *Age*, 10 May 1997.
4 'Dear John . . .', *Age*, 24 March 1997.
5 Ibid.
6 'Stand firm on Wik, Howard urged', *Age*, 21 April 1997; our italics.
7 'Wik a nightmare in Howard's Dreamtime', *Age*, 22 April 1997.
8 'Is this really one Australia for all Australians?', *Weekend Australian*, 21–22 August 1993.
9 Ibid.

Bibliography

Books, Journals and Reports

Anderson, Campbell. 'Need for more micro-economic reform', *Mining Review*, vol. 15, 1991, p. 7.

Anderson, Christopher. 'Aboriginal people and museums: restricting access to increase it', *Art Link*, vol. 12, 1991, pp. 11–12.

—— 'Australian Aborigines and museums—a new relationship', *Curator*, vol. 33, 1990, pp. 173–4.

—— 'The economies of sacred art: the uses of a secret collection in the South Australian Museum', in C. Anderson (ed.), *Politics of the Secret: Oceania Monograph*, vol. 45, University of Sydney/Oceania Publications, Sydney 1995, p. 101.

Anon. 'Sorting out the mess that's Territory mining', *Australia's Mining Monthly*, October 1992, p. 39.

Arndt, Walter. 'The Nargorkun-Narlinji cult', *Oceania*, vol. 32, 1962, pp. 298–320.

Australian Mining Industry Council. *Shrinking Australia: Australia's Economic Future: Access to Land.* Australian Mining Industry Council, Dickson, ACT 1990.

Bataille, Georges. *The Accursed Share*, trans. Robert Hurley. Zone Books, New York (1967) 1991.

Benjamin, Walter. 'The Storyteller', *Illuminations*, trans. Harry Zohn, Fontana, London (1936) 1973.

—— 'Unpacking My Library', *Illuminations*, trans. Harry Zohn, Fontana, London (1931) 1973.

Berndt, Ronald M. and Berndt, Catherine H. *The World of the First Australians.* Aboriginal Studies Press, Canberra (1964) 1988.

Brunton, Ron. *A Weak Defence: Anthropologists Fail to Salvage the Resource Assessments Commission's Kakadu Report.* Institute of Public Affairs, Canberra 1991.

—— 'Aborigines and environmental myths: Apocalypse in Kakadu', *Environmental Backgrounder*, Institute of Public Affairs, Canberra 1991.

—— 'Controversy in the Sickness Country: the battle over Coronation Hill', *Quadrant*, vol. 35, 1991, pp. 16–20.

—— *The Significance of Shallow Traditions: The Resource Assessment Commission on Aboriginal Interests in Kakadu.* Institute of Public Affairs, Canberra 1991.

—— *Blocking Business: An Anthropological Assessment of the Hindmarsh Island Dispute.* Tasman Institute Occasional Paper B31, Melbourne 1995.

Carroll, John. 'Howard's forgotten people', *The Australian's Review of Books*, December 1996–January 1997, p. 32.

Central Land Council, Pitjantjatjara Council and the Mutitjulu Community. *Sharing the Park: Anangu Initiatives in Ayers Rock Tourism.* Institute for Aboriginal Development, Alice Springs 1991.

Cochrane, Peter. 'Race memory', *The Australian's Review of Books*, November 1996, pp. 8–9, 30.

Cooper, D. *Report for the Registration of the Upper South Alligator Bula Complex.* Aboriginal Sacred Sites Protection Authority, Darwin 1985.

Copjec, Joan. *Read My Desire: Lacan Against the Historicists.* MIT Press, Cambridge, Mass. 1994.

Davis, S. L. and Prescott, J. R. V. *Aboriginal Frontiers and Boundaries in Australia.* Melbourne University Press, Carlton 1992.

Davis, S. L., Resource Managers Pty Ltd and the Australian Mining Industry Council. *Australia's Extant and Imputed Traditional Aboriginal Territories.* Melbourne University Press, Carlton 1993.

Derrida, Jacques. 'Différance', *Margins of Philosophy.* Harvester Wheatsheaf, Hertfordshire 1982.

Dienst, Richard. *Still Life in Real Time: Theory After Television.* Duke University Press, Durham and London 1994.

Durkheim, Emile. *The Elementary Forms of the Religious Life*, trans. Joseph Ward Swain, George Allen & Unwin, London (1915) 1976.

Elkin, A. P. *Aboriginal Men of High Degree.* Australasian Publishing, Sydney 1945.

Fanon, Frantz. *Black Skin, White Masks*, trans. Charles Lam Markmann, Grove Press, New York (1952) 1967.

Freud, Sigmund. 'The "Uncanny"', in A. Dickson (ed.), *The Pelican Freud Library: Art and Literature*, vol. 14, Penguin Books, Harmondsworth (1919) 1987, pp. 342–7.

Gibson, Ross. *South of the West: Postcolonialism and the Narrative Construction of Australia.* Indiana University Press, Bloomington and Indianapolis 1992.

Gough, Austin. 'Hindmarsh Island and the politics of the future', *Adelaide Review*, June 1995, pp. 3–4.

Grey, Tony. *Jabiluka: The Battle to Mine Australia's Uranium.* Text Publishing, Melbourne 1994.

Griffiths, Tom. *Hunters and Collectors: The Antiquarian Imagination in Australia*. Cambridge University Press, Cambridge 1996.

Hall, Stuart. 'When was "the post-colonial"? Thinking at the limit', in I. Chambers and L. Curti (eds), *The Post-Colonial Question: Common Skies, Divided Horizons*. Routledge, London and New York 1996.

Hawke, Steve. *Noonkanbah: Whose Land, Whose Laws*. Fremantle Arts Centre Press, Fremantle 1989.

Hill, Barry. *The Rock: Travelling to Uluru*. Allen & Unwin, Sydney 1994.

Hollier, Denis (ed.). *The College of Sociology (1937–39)*, trans. by Betsy Wing, University of Minnesota Press, Minneapolis 1989.

Howard, John. 'Restore the fairness for families', *Age*, 5 September 1997.

Jeater, Diana. 'Roast beef and reggae music: the passing of whiteness', *New Formations*, vol. 18, 1992, pp. 107–21.

Johnson, Vivien. 'Poetic justice', *Art & Text*, vol. 42, 1992, pp. 34–6.

Keen, Ian and Merlan, Francesca. *The Significance of the Conservation Zone to Aboriginal People*. Resource Assessment Commission, Kakadu Conservation Zone Inquiry Consultancy Series. Australian Government Printing Service, Canberra 1990.

Kelly, Ray. 'Why we bother', in K. Brereton (ed.), *Australian Mythological Sights: Sites: Cites*, Third Degree, Sydney 1986, pp. 99–100.

Kenny, Chris. *'It Would Be Nice if There was Some Women's Business': The Story Behind the Hindmarsh Island Affair*. Duffy & Snellgrove, Potts Point 1995.

Kristeva, Julia. *Strangers to Ourselves*, trans. Leon S. Roudiez, Columbia University Press, New York 1991.

Langton, Marcia. *'Well, I Heard it on the Radio and I Saw it on the Television . . .'*. Australian Film Commission, North Sydney 1993.

Lattas, Andrew. 'Aborigines and contemporary Australian nationalism: primordiality and the cultural politics of otherness', in J. Marcus (ed.), *Writing Australian Culture: Text, Society and National Identity*, special issue, *Social Analysis: Journal of Cultural and Social Practice*, vol. 27, 1990, pp. 50–69.

Leiris, Michel. 'The sacred in everyday life', in D. Hollier (ed.), *The College of Sociology (1937–39)*, trans. by Betsy Wing, University of Minnesota Press, Minneapolis 1989.

Lyotard, Jean-Francois. *The Differend: Phrases in Dispute*, trans. Georges Van Den Abbeele, University of Minnesota Press, Minneapolis 1988.

McIntosh, Lauchlan. 'Land access and the shrinking world of mining', *Mining Review*, vol. 11, November 1987, p. 7.

Maddock, Kenneth. 'God, Caesar and Mammon at Coronation Hill', *Oceania*, vol. 58, 1988, pp. 305–10.

—— 'Metamorphosing the sacred in Australia', *Australian Journal of Anthropology*, vol. 2, 1991, pp. 213–32.

—— 'Yet another "sacred site": the Bula controversy', in B. Wright, G. Fry and L. Petchkovsky (eds), *Contemporary Issues in Aboriginal Studies:*

Proceedings of the First Nepean Conference on Aboriginal Studies. Firebird Press, Sydney 1987, pp. 119–40.

—— *Your Land is Our Land: Aboriginal Land Rights.* Penguin, Melbourne 1983.

Marcus, Julie. 'The journey out to the Centre: the cultural appropriation of Ayers Rock', in A. Rutherford (ed.), *Aboriginal Culture Today*, Dangaroo Press, Sydney 1988.

Mauss, Marcel. *The Gift: The Form and Reason for Exchange in Archaic Societies*, trans. W.D. Halls. Routledge, London (1950) 1990.

Mead, Greg. *A Royal Omission: A Critical Summary of the Evidence Given to the Hindmarsh Island Bridge Royal Commission with an Alternative Report.* Greg Mead, Adelaide 1995.

Merlan, Francesca. 'The limits of cultural constructionism: the case of Coronation Hill', *Oceania*, vol. 61, 1991, pp. 341–52.

Morgan, Hugh. 'The dire implications of Coronation Hill', *IPA Review*, vol. 44, 1991, pp. 36–7.

Morris, Meaghan. *The Pirate's Fiancée: Feminism, Reading, Post-modernism.* Verso, London and New York 1988.

Muecke, Stephen. *Textual Spaces: Aboriginality and Cultural Studies.* New South Wales University Press, Sydney 1992.

Mulvaney, D. J. 'Past regained, future lost: the Kow Swamp Pleistocene burials', *Antiquity*, vol. 65N, 1991, pp. 12–21.

Mumbulla, Percy. 'The Bunyip', in K. Gelder (ed.), *The Oxford Book of Australian Ghost Stories*. Oxford University Press, Melbourne 1994, pp. 250–1.

Murray, Tim. 'Aborigines, archaeology and Australian heritage', *Meanjin*, vol. 55, 1996, pp. 725–35.

O'Loughlin, Judge Maurice. *Chapman and Others v. Tickner and Others, Federal Court Reports* 1995.

Pardoe, Colin. 'Arches of Radii, corridors of power: reflections on current archaeological practice', *Journal of Australian Studies*, vol. 35, 1992, pp. 132–41.

Praed, Rosa Campbell. 'The Bunyip', in K. Gelder (ed.), *The Oxford Book of Australian Ghost Stories*. Oxford University Press, Melbourne 1994, pp. 102–9.

Raynor, Mark. 'Uncertainty: risks in decision making', *Mining Review*, vol. 16, May 1992, p. 25.

Read, Peter. *Returning to Nothing: The Meaning of Lost Places.* Cambridge University Press, Cambridge 1996.

Readings, Bill. *Introducing Lyotard: Art and Politics.* Routledge, London 1991.

Richardson, Michael. *Georges Bataille*, Routledge, London 1994.

Roberts, Jim (dir.). *Sacred Journey* (documentary). Mills Street Productions Pty Ltd./Australian Broadcasting Corporation 1996.

Rowse, Tim. 'Hosts and guests at Uluru', *Meanjin*, vol. 51, 1992, pp. 247–58.

—— 'Mabo and moral anxiety', *Meanjin*, vol. 52, 1993, pp. 229–52.

Stevens, Iris E. *Report of the Hindmarsh Island Royal Commission*, State Print, Adelaide 1995.

Tacey, David. *Edge of the Sacred: Transformation in Australia*. HarperCollins, North Blackburn, Victoria 1995.

Taussig, Michael. *The Nervous System*. Routledge, London and New York 1994.

Thomas, Nicholas. *Colonialism's Culture: Anthropology, Travel and Government*. Melbourne University Press, Carlton 1994.

Watson, Sam. 'I say this to you' (interview), *Meanjin*, vol. 53, 1994, pp. 589–96.

—— *The Kadaitcha Sung*. Penguin Books, Ringwood 1990.

Welatye-Therre Defence Committee. *Voices from Mparntwe*. Welatye-Therre Defence Committee Broadsheet, Alice Springs n.d.

Wharton, Herb. *Where Ya' Been, Mate*. University of Queensland Press, St Lucia, Brisbane 1996.

Williams, Raymond. 'Dominant, residual, and emergent', *Marxism and Literature*. Oxford University Press, Oxford 1977.

Wilson, Dulcie. 'Telling the truth', *IPA Review*, vol. 49, 1996, pp. 39–40.

Wootton, Justice Hal. *Significant Aboriginal Sites in Areas of Proposed Junction Waterhole Dam, Alice Springs. Report to the Minister for Aboriginal Affairs*. Aboriginal and Torres Strait Islander Commission, Canberra 1992.

Newspaper Articles

'Blacks fight plan to flood sacred site', *Age*, 22 April 1983.

'Coronation Hill may be PM's answer to his son', *Age*, 18 June 1991.

'Coronation Hill test for sacred sites', *Australian*, 9 May 1991.

'Dear John . . .', *Age*, 24 March 1997.

'Digging for an excuse', *Herald Sun*, 28 May 1991.

'Doing battle in a land long shared', *Age*, 9 June 1997.

Editorial, *Australian*, 11 December 1995.

'Hostages to a Bula legend', *Australian*, 2 May 1991.

'If we get MABO wrong. We'll all lose, again' (advertisement), *Sydney Morning Herald*, 6 August 1993.

'Is this really one Australia for all Australians?', *Weekend Australian*, 21–22 August 1993.

'Kerin exalts Coronation Hill as "totem issue" for business', *Australian Financial Review*, 12 June 1991.

'Liberty taken with the legends', *Sunday Herald*, 5 August 1990.

'Lies, lies, lies', *Advertiser*, 22 December 1995.

'Mabo scaremongers distort truth with statistics', *Sydney Morning Herald*, 2 February 1994.

'Mungo woman back to the dreamtime', *Age*, 18 January 1992.

'Mungo woman returns to her people', *Age*, 13 January 1992.

'Not just a sacred site, also a political totem', *Age*, 20 June 1991.

'Race to the polls raises questions of Katter's "racist" remarks', *Age*, 28 February 1996.

'Racism row distracts Liberals', *Age*, 28 February 1996.

'Rationality is fine, when it suits us', *Canberra Times*, 26 March 1995.

'Ruling fails to end title conflict', *Age*, 24 December 1996.

'SA poised to probe bridge saga', *Advertiser*, 8 June 1995.

'Scientist appeals for fair Deal', *Age*, 21 October 1996.

'Secrets to stay sealed', *Advertiser*, 2 November 1995.

'Shame of the nation', *Age*, 28 August 1995.

'"Sickness Country" may become a national epidemic', *Weekend Australian*, 22–23 June 1991.

'Stand firm on Wik, Howard urged', *Age*, 21 April 1997.

'The effect on the Jawoyn outweighs economic benefit', *Australian Financial Review*, 19 June 1991.

'The New Racists are in charge', *Herald Sun*, 29 February 1996.

'When bad omens come in boats', *Age*, 11 January 1997.

'Who are the Wik winners?' *Age*, 10 May 1997.

'Wik a nightmare in Howard's Dreamtime', *Age*, 22 April 1997.

Index